MW01046308

the smartdiet

Better Homes and Gardens® Books • Des Moines, Iowa

Better Homes and Gardens® Books
An imprint of Meredith® Books

the smartdiet

Editor: Kristi M. Fuller, R.D.
Senior Associate Design Director: Richard Michels
Contributing Editors: Linda Henry, Jan Miller, R.D.
Contributing Writers: Bev Bennett; Diane Quagliani, R.D.;
 Marcia Kay Stanley, R.D.; Terri Wolf
Additional Contributors: Monika M. Woolsey, R.D; Evelyn Tribole, R.D.;
 Dayle Hayes, R.D.
Photographer: Mark Thomas
Food Stylist: William Smith
Prop Stylists: Nancy Micklin
Illustrator: Lisa Henderling
Copy Chief: Catherine Hamrick
Copy and Production Editor: Terri Fredrickson
Managers, Book Production: Pam Kvitne, Marjorie J. Schenkelberg
Contributing Copy Editors: Garland Walton, Shirley Williams
Contributing Proofreaders: Maria Duryee, Jacquelyn Foster, Marcy Hall,
 Gretchen Kauffman, Amy Ritt
Electronic Production Coordinator: Paula Forest
Editorial and Design Assistants: Judy Bailey, Mary Lee Gavin, Karen Schirm
Test Kitchen Director: Lynn Blanchard
Test Kitchen Product Supervisor: Marilyn Cornelius

MEREDITH® BOOKS
Editor in Chief: James D. Blume
Design Director: Matt Strelecki
Managing Editor: Gregory H. Kayko
Executive Food Editor: Jennifer Dorland Darling

Director, Retail Sales and Marketing: Terry Unsworth
Director, Sales, Special Markets: Rita McMullen
Director, Sales, Home & Garden Centers: Ray Wolf
Director, Sales, Premiums: Michael A. Peterson
Director, Sales, Retail: Tom Wierzbicki
Director, Book Marketing: Brad Elmitt
Director, Operations: George A. Susral
Director, Production: Douglas M. Johnston
Vice President, General Manager: Jamie L. Martin

BETTER HOMES AND GARDENS® MAGAZINE
Editor in Chief: Jean LemMon
Executive Food Editor: Nancy Byal

MEREDITH PUBLISHING GROUP
President, Publishing Group: Christopher M. Little
Vice President, Finance & Administration: Max Runciman

MEREDITH CORPORATION
Chairman and Chief Executive Officer: William T. Kerr
Chairman of the Executive Committee: E. T. Meredith III

Copyright © 2000 by Meredith
Corporation, Des Moines, Iowa.
All rights reserved. Printed
in the United States of America.
First Edition—00
Library of Congress Catalog Control
Number: 00-133275
ISBN: 0-696-21173-4

All of us at Better Homes and
Gardens® Books are dedicated to
providing you with the information
and ideas you need to create
delicious foods. We welcome your
comments and suggestions. Write
to us at: Better Homes and Gardens
Books, Cookbook Editorial
Department, 1716 Locust St.,
Des Moines, IA 50309-3023.

If you would like to purchase
any of our books, check
wherever quality books are sold.
Visit our website at bhg.com or
bhgbooks.com

Our seal assures you that every
recipe in *The Smart Diet* has been
tested in the Better Homes and
Gardens® Test Kitchen. This means
that each recipe is practical and
reliable, and meets our high
standards of taste appeal. We
guarantee your satisfaction with
this book for as long as you own it.

Diet (dī'-ət) n : food or drink regularly provided or consumed; habitual nourishment.

Is this your definition of the word "diet"? Or, do words such as "restrictive," "boring," "bland," "spartan," and "deprived" come to mind?

Take a moment to think about your dieting history. Have you followed one or more of the popular fad diets? Did you keep the weight off? Perhaps you lost weight and gained back every pound—and then some. If this has been your experience, it's time to evolve to a smarter way of thinking about food, your weight, and yourself. This is what *Better Homes and Gardens® The Smart Diet* is all about.

give up dieting forever

FINDING A BETTER WAY

The Smart Diet introduces you to a different way of thinking about your weight, what you eat, and how you exercise. It's called the "nondiet" approach, and, yes, it involves giving up diets and renegotiating your image of an attractive body. At its core, the nondiet approach is about nurturing all facets of your life: physical, emotional, mental, and spiritual. The ideology of this concept is summarized in "Principles of a Nondiet Approach" (*far right*).

You will learn more about these principles and explore how to incorporate them into your lifestyle. You will also read advice from experts and real people who stopped dieting and not only survived, but also thrived. (See "Nondieters' Success Stories," *page* 8.)

By the end of this section, we hope you'll adopt a new definition of the word diet—and agree that the smartest diet is no diet at all.

A LOSING BATTLE?

If you diet repeatedly only to have the weight creep back on, you are not alone. An estimated 95 percent of people who lose weight by dieting gain back the weight within five years. Many people add a few more pounds on top of that.

About one in three American adults tries to lose weight at any given time. They spend more than $30 billion each year on diet products, programs, potions, powders, and pills. You would think Americans would be the most svelte people in the world. Yet the number of people in the United States who are overweight or obese is steadily climbing. In fact, it is estimated that about half of all U.S. adults fall into one these two categories.

Something doesn't add up. Maybe you think that people—yourself included—fail on diets because they lack willpower or just haven't found the right plan for them. Here's a new way to look at it: Could it be that diets are failing them? Do diets just not work? Yes, say a growing number of nutrition experts and people like you. In fact, they say the route to feeling happy about your body—and yourself—is to stop dieting altogether.

THE DIET TRAP

It's hard to resist the allure of diets. Our culture is mesmerized by thinness. From an early age, we see slender images splashed across billboards and gracing TV shows, advertisements, movies, and magazines. Ironically, even those waiflike models need an airbrushing before they're deemed page-worthy. How is the average person supposed to attain that? No wonder we're a diet-mad society, so willing to pin our hopes on every latest fad diet that comes along. Diets set unrealistic expectations that are as elusive as the proverbial carrot on a stick.

THE ALLURE OF BEING THIN

Consider what you think losing weight will do for you. Sure, you expect to get thinner, but how do you imagine your life to be then? Will you find your dream love match? Get a promotion? Be more popular? Enjoy great wealth? If you think you'll finally have the perfect life and feel terrific about yourself, you have lots of company. "Our society is obsessed with thinness and promotes weight loss as the key to happiness and the answer to many of life's problems," says registered dietitian Dayle Hayes, an

PRINCIPLES OF A NONDIET APPROACH

• Focus on your total health and well-being, including mind, body, and spirit, instead of focusing on weight loss or striving to reach an unrealistic weight.

• Respect and accept the diversity of the physical attributes of your own body as well as the bodies of others.

• Develop a true awareness of the pleasures of eating—rely on internal hunger cues.

• Enjoy a variety of foods rather than rely on limiting diets or strict meal plans.

• Celebrate the joy of physical activity. Include a wide array of activities, rather than follow rigid routines or regimented exercises.

• Honor and love yourself fully and authentically.

advocate of the nondiet approach, author, and nutrition therapist in Billings, Montana. These promises are seductive, but seldom, if ever, come true. You can probably lose weight on any diet, but you'll still be the same person. "Once the initial thrill of buying new clothes in a smaller size wears off, you still face the same set of problems you had before you lost weight," says Hayes. Weight loss never changes who you really are, nor will it make you happy. Happiness is internal.

WHY DIETS FAIL

Many discouraging statistics report that people who lose weight on a diet will gain it back within a few years. One reason for this dismal success rate is that people often view diets as a temporary situation to endure until they lose weight. Then they go off the diet and back to the same eating patterns that caused them to gain weight.

Another reason diets are unsuccessful is that they override inborn hunger and fullness signals, placing external controls on eating. "Chronic dieters are used to eating when, what, and how much their current diet dictates, not because they're hungry or full," says registered dietitian Evelyn Tribole, a southern California-based weight management and eating disorders specialist.

Eventually dieters are compelled to break the rigid food rules, which often results in rebound overeating. "Diets backfire because they're so restrictive," says Tribole. "The more dieters restrict food, the more likely they'll overeat when they break the diet, and they'll gain back any weight they've lost."

More discouraging is that on many diets, especially those that produce fast weight loss, muscle mass is lost along with fat stores. When those pounds are regained, they come back mostly as fat. "You may end up weighing the same, but you'll have a higher percentage of body fat," says Hayes. In addition, repeated dieting plays havoc with the metabolism by decreasing the number of calories needed to perform basic functions such as breathing and digestion. This means fewer calories are needed to maintain weight, and eventually weight is gained more easily.

Consider health and safety. Some diets advocate eating plans that are based on faulty claims and the elimination of certain foods. For example, the current rage is high-protein, low-carbohydrate diets, which ban or severely limit fruits, vegetables, and grains—the very foods that sound scientific research shows can enhance your health and help prevent chronic diseases. Healthy, tantalizing food can and should be part of your diet! The recipes in *The Smart Diet* will help you discover the pleasures of eating delicious food again.

THE FOLLY OF FAD DIETS

You've heard the advertisements that make fabulous claims of fast and effortless weight loss. Maybe you've tried more than a few of these weight-loss schemes yourself. In the long run, fad diets don't deliver on their promises—and any pounds that may have disappeared are soon back with a vengeance. Here are the facts about three popular types of fad diets.

High-Protein, Low-Carbohydrate Diets
The premise: There are several variations of this type of diet. The carbohydrates in foods such as

WHAT'S WRONG WITH THIS PICTURE?

The perception of the ideal body has become distorted due to the media's emphasis on unnaturally thin models and actors. If you're striving to meet this super-thin ideal, consider this:

• The average woman in the U.S. is 5'4" tall, weighs 142 pounds, and wears size 12 to 14.

• 30 million U.S. women wear size 16 or larger.

• The average fashion model is 5'9" tall, weighs 110 pounds, and wears a size 6 or 8.

breads, cereals, rice, pastas, fruits, and vegetables are blamed for weight gain because (take your pick) people are "allergic" to them, "addicted" to them, or because eating carbohydrates causes insulin resistance, which makes the body store fat.

The promise: Burn fat stores and lose weight by feasting on high-protein (and often high-fat) foods such as steaks, burgers, cheeses, and eggs and eliminating or severely restricting carbohydrate-containing foods.

The facts: There is no scientific evidence that carbohydrates are the villains they are made out to be. In fact, carbohydrates are essential for good health. Rapid initial weight loss can occur on these diets as your body taps into its carbohydrate stores for the fuel it thrives on. Initial losses are mostly water and some precious muscle mass. (Remember: The more muscle mass you have, the more calories you burn doing nothing.) Curtailing carbohydrates also can throw your body into a state of ketosis, a result of an incomplete metabolism of fatty acids due to a carbohydrate deficiency. This same state is seen with diabetes, where carbohydrates can't be utilized properly. Ketosis taxes your kidneys and causes a fruity breath odor. If you do lose weight on this diet, it's because your food choices are so limited that you consume fewer calories, not because you've forsaken carbohydrates.

Eating more than your body needs of any food, whether it predominately consists of carbohydrates, proteins, or fats, will cause fat storage and weight gain. Also, insulin resistance does not cause the body to store fat. Instead, being overweight often causes insulin resistance. This condition stimulates the pancreas to produce large amounts of insulin because the body can't effectively use normal quantities of insulin to handle the amount of glucose in the blood after eating. Carbohydrates aren't the villains as implicated.

The bottom line is that many health experts discourage high-protein, low-carbohydrate diets that eliminate health-enhancing foods and are difficult to adhere to. Fortunately, many people only flirt briefly with these diets because they soon tire of the narrow food choices and accompanying complaints, such as constipation, headache, fatigue, or nausea. In light of all of the research that has uncovered the many health benefits of eating a diet high in fruits and vegetables, it doesn't make sense to shortchange yourself.

Food Combining Diets

The premise: Eating foods containing carbohydrates, protein, and fat at the same meal causes your body to store fat because your enzymes can't properly digest these nutrient combinations.

The promise: Eat foods in specific combinations (e.g., never eat protein foods with carbohydrate foods; always eat fruit by itself), and weight loss will follow.

The facts: A healthy body is capable of digesting any combination of foods. Eating fruits separately from other foods actually can shortchange your health. For instance, the vitamin C abundant in many fruits, such as oranges and grapefruits, enhances the absorption of iron from foods such as meat and spinach. In addition, eating a combination of carbohydrates,

Continued on page 9

PLOT YOUR PERSONAL DIET TIMELINE

For each diet you've tried, write down which one it was, when you were on it, how much it cost, how many pounds you lost, and, most important, what happened to your weight once you stopped the diet.

"Most people see that sooner or later their weight climbs back up after each diet," says registered dietitian Dayle Hayes. "It's a real eye-opener that convinces people once and for all that diets don't work for them."

Carolyn, 47, is a high school teacher who lives in Denver. Considered chubby as a child, she started dieting at age 12. Thus began a nearly 20-year diet saga. "I tried **"Food is not the center of the universe."** nearly every diet known to man and nearly 'tuna-ed' myself to death," says Carolyn. "My eating was chaotic and compulsive. It was heartbreaking to see my weight go up." Also, she was a devoted couch potato. At age 35, her weight topped off at 232 pounds and she wore a size 20+. That's when she embarked on the nondiet approach with the help of a registered dietitian. Over the years, Carolyn has lost nearly 30 pounds and wears a size 16. She now enjoys daily physical activity and describes herself as "really fit."

Pam, 26, a buyer for a clothing store, has always battled her weight. She has suffered much guilt about being overweight and constantly obsesses about her choices of foods. "One of the many foods I often felt guilty about eating was pizza. I discussed these feelings with my dietitian friend, who asked me to explain to her what was wrong with pizza. She also asked me to tell her what was good about **"I started focusing on the good things about foods."** pizza—the positive aspects of pizza." Pam began to see that pizza did have some good qualities, especially when it's loaded with vegetables. "When I started focusing on the good things about foods I was eating, I stopped obsessing about how 'bad' I was."

Gary, 40, a stockbroker in Connecticut, is 5'10" tall and 200 pounds. According to the Body Mass Index (BMI), which is often used to determine a person's "appropriate" weight, Gary is in the overweight **"I'd rather eat the things I enjoy than obsess about my weight."** category (a BMI of 27.8 or more for men). Gary works out at the gym at least four times a week and is muscular. He is very active and eats a somewhat healthy diet. "I have a passion for ice cream, which I eat several times a week." Although he does not look overweight, he laments about his love handles. "I know if I stopped eating ice cream, they'd go away; but I enjoy ice cream and I don't want to give it up. So, I'll live with love handles."

NONDIETERS' SUCCESS STORIES

Susan, 33, a copy editor in California, has dieted constantly since she was a teenager. Her struggle with weight **"I'm at a weight that is comfortable to me."** continued after her marriage. "Having two children within a few years of each other didn't help matters. As my children got older, dieting suddenly wasn't as important. I had a family to worry about, and I decided I didn't want them growing up obsessing about their weight." Susan implemented a healthier diet for herself and her family. She started walking after dinner with her husband and kids. She never felt deprived with her new way of eating, and she felt better. The biggest shocker to Susan was that she began losing weight without dieting.

Julianne, 45, is an attorney who lives in Chicago. Since her teens, she's tried to manage her weight by counting calories, shunning "fattening" foods, and exercising "fanatically." These periods were followed by episodes of bingeing and weight gain. Over the years, her weight has bobbed up and down. She hit a high of 189 pounds after her freshman year in college and a low of 117 pounds in her mid-thirties following a strict diet and **"I'm taking care of myself."** rigorous exercise program. "That low lasted for about five minutes," she says. Four years ago a friend recommended a book on the nondiet approach. Since then, her bingeing has gradually subsided, and she's more relaxed about food, exercise, and her weight.

Karen, 41, an editor in Des Moines, appeared to be healthy at the age of 36. At 5'5" tall, 120 pounds, and a size 4, she looked like what many women aspire to be. The **"I was thin but unfit."** reality was she wasn't healthy. "I didn't exercise and my diet wasn't the best either. I was stressed out, unhappy, and had bad skin and thin hair. A major health scare turned me around." Karen began exercising at least three times a week and started to eat a more nutritious diet. After several months of exercising, Karen gained 13 pounds and her clothing went up a size. "At age 41, my skin is clearer than it has ever been, my hair is healthier, and I have muscle tone in my once-flabby thighs. Frequent exercise also has made a difference in my attitude."

Continued from page 7

proteins, and fats at meals helps you maintain a steady energy level and feel satisfied longer.

Fat Burning Foods

The premise: Certain foods can burn away body fat.

The promise: Eat all of the _____ (fill in the blank) you want—and only that particular food—and watch the pounds melt away.

The facts: No food stimulates your body to burn fat. These diets seem to work initially as you eat unlimited quantities and lose weight. Weight loss occurs because the "fat-burning" food is usually quite low in calories. You lose weight because you're eating fewer total calories, not because the food is magically burning away body fat. These diets are nutritionally unbalanced and risky for your health. Fortunately, most people soon give up because they're quickly bored with eating one type of food.

FOOD FOR THOUGHT: ARE YOU READY TO STOP DIETING?

Perhaps you now believe that diets don't work. If you have been dieting for years, it's not easy to stop. Ask yourself these questions to see if you're ready to banish diets from your life and embrace the principles of the nondiet approach. Answering "yes" to even one question makes you a likely candidate.

• Are you unable to face starting a new diet? If you don't have the energy or motivation to even think about it, you're ready for a new approach.

• Do you want to enjoy and feel relaxed around food in any situation rather than obsess about how many calories you eat, deciding whether you should or shouldn't eat a certain food, and feeling guilty when you do eat something not on your diet?

• Do you wish to break free from a cycle of food restriction and the bingeing that often follows? Once dieting stops, compulsive behaviors often begin to heal and eating patterns normalize.

• Do you eat when you're not hungry to soothe or mask your emotions, or to distract yourself from your problems? You can learn to deal with life's issues and care for yourself without food.

• Are you ready to focus on your health and well-being rather than your weight? Can you begin to love yourself with a body that is not perfect? It's difficult to make healthy choices in your life when you constantly tell yourself you're fat, disgusting, and out of control.

• Are you ready to experience life now and stop putting life on hold until you lose weight? Can you accept that learning and living the nondiet approach is a lifelong process, not a temporary quick fix?

WILL YOU LOSE WEIGHT BY FOLLOWING THE NONDIET APPROACH?

You're probably wondering what will happen to your weight when you stop dieting. Will you lose weight? Yes, if you've been overeating and underactive. There's no guarantee, however, says registered dietitian Monika Woolsey, president of A Better Way Health Consulting, Inc. in Glendale, Arizona, and publisher of *After the Diet*, a newsletter for health professionals who specialize in weight and

Q AND A

Q: *What if it's an eating disorder?*

A: Coping with emotional issues by bingeing or eating when you're not hungry may signal an eating disorder. For help, talk with a trusted doctor, mental health counselor, or registered dietitian. These online resources also can help:

"The Something Fishy Website on Eating Disorders" at something-fishy.org provides comprehensive information on eating disorders.

The website for "Eating Disorders Awareness and Prevention" at edap.org provides information on identifying eating disorders and promoting a healthy body image.

eating issues. "If your current weight is more than your body is naturally programmed to be, you'll probably lose weight until you settle at your natural weight," says Woolsey. "If you think you're overweight when you're not, your weight will either stay the same, or you might even gain until you reach your natural weight." If you do lose weight, odds are you'll shed it slowly, which means you're apt to keep it off.

Your natural weight (and the weight that's probably healthy for you) is the weight at which your body settles when you consistently eat enough food to nourish yourself, honor your inner signals of hunger and fullness, and don't use external measures such as diets and exercise to control weight.

Breaking free from dieting and accepting a weight that's higher than you have always hoped for isn't easy, especially in our "thin is in" society. Respecting your body enough to let it take on its genetic shape is a critical step in developing a more relaxed and enjoyable relationship with food and with yourself.

STEPS TOWARD FREEDOM FROM DIETS

"Resources" (*left*) lists helpful books and websites that contain more in-depth information on the nondiet approach. These resources employ a common core of shedding rigid diet rules, making peace with food, and respecting and honoring yourself and your body as it is.

Begin with the basic steps. Start with the ideas that feel right to you and move to the next step at your own pace. Gently explore these options and be patient with yourself. If you've dieted for years, you'll need time to free yourself—physically and mentally—from the clutches of dieting. Remember, this is a lifelong process, not a temporary quick fix.

Congratulate yourself for each small step you take along the path to a healthy, happy, diet-free lifestyle.

View foods as equals.

Food is for fuel, nourishment, and enjoyment. Avoid classifying foods as "good" or "bad," "OK to eat," or "off-limits." Instead, allow yourself to eat the foods you want. (Of course, you should avoid foods you're allergic to or can't tolerate for health reasons.) Nondiet proponents term lifting the ban on certain foods as "legalizing, neutralizing, or equalizing" foods and say it's a key step to break away from the diet/binge cycle.

When you try to banish your favorite snack food, candy, or dessert, you probably crave it most. Tribole says food restrictions lead to "Last Supper" eating: overeating triggered by anticipated deprivation. It can feel scary to allow yourself to eat the foods you struggled to avoid. Ironically, though, granting yourself guilt-free permission to eat forbidden foods often extinguishes the desire to eat them. If you occasionally eat too much, so what? People of average weight do that, too, and they don't give it a second thought.

Tune in to your natural hunger and fullness signals.

"Many people are used to having portion sizes determined for them, either by the diet they've been on or by what's served to them in a restaurant," says Woolsey. It takes some time, and with patience and gentle persistence, you can get in touch with your inner signals. "Generally, your body needs food

RESOURCES

These books and websites provide information on the nondiet approach and developing a healthy relationship with food:

Intuitive Eating
Evelyn Tribole, M.S., R.D., and Elyse Resch, M.S., R.D., St. Martin's Paperbacks, 1995.

It's Not About Food
Carol Emery Normandi and Laurelee Roark, Grosset/Putnam, 1998.

Overcoming Overeating
Jane R. Hirschmann and Carol H. Munter, Fawcett Columbine, 1988.

The Solution
Laurel Mellin, M.A., R.D., ReganBooks/Harper Collins, 1997.

hugs.com
overcomingovereating.com
afterthediet.com
bodypositive.com

about every five hours," says Tribole. "Check in with yourself throughout the day to detect hunger." Eventually, listening and responding to your inner signals will become natural.

Eat breakfast.

You might be used to skipping breakfast to cut calories, but that ploy backfires because you most likely feel famished—and probably overeat—later in the day. "Skipping breakfast deprives you of the energy kickstart you need each morning," says Woolsey. "Your body spends the rest of the day playing catch-up to regain its energy equilibrium." If you're not hungry first thing in the morning, that's OK. Eat when you get to work or tote something healthful with you to eat on the run. Some foods to take along include yogurt and fresh fruit.

Explore emotional eating.

If you use food, diets, and weight obsession to mask your feelings and distract yourself from the real issues in your life, look inside yourself to discover your true needs. Keep a food and mood journal to uncover patterns of eating when you're not hungry. Write down when, what, and how much you eat, how hungry you are when you start and stop eating, and what you feel.

If you want to eat even though you're not hungry or you keep eating when you're full, figure out what you really need. For instance, if you're tired, take a short nap or break; if you're lonely, call a friend; if you feel stressed, take a five-minute walk. Put yourself and your needs first.

Cultivate an appreciative and adventurous palate.

When you savor well-prepared foods, you may be satisfied with less, especially when you're free to eat any food you like. Eating low-calorie or fat-free "diet" foods temporarily fools your hunger but rates low on taste and satisfaction. So you eat more of these substitutes and maybe more calories than if you enjoyed the real thing. Cultivate a selective palate that demands only the best-tasting, highest-quality foods. Before you eat, pause to ask yourself what you really want. Making that match is enjoyable and means you're taking care of yourself.

Expand your food horizons.

Experiment with the recipes in this book for exciting meals to look forward to. Enroll in cooking classes and learn the adventures of using new spices, herbs, and seasonings in cooking. It will teach you the art and pleasure of food, giving you a new appreciation for foods you choose to put into your body.

Keep a gratitude journal.

Each day, record five blessings in your life. You have plenty to be thankful for—a home, a loving family, good friends, a job, a sunny day, the knowledge you've acquired, even having a warm coat. Many people don't have these things. Remember to express gratitude for your body and all the remarkable things it does for you. A mind that counts blessings has no room for self-pity.

Talk yourself into higher self-esteem.

Positive self talk can urge you to greater heights. If you have trouble thinking positively, and are often plagued by negative thoughts, look into your past for sources of low self-esteem. Retrieve critical comments that were made to you, especially as a child. If necessary, talk to a counselor to help you

Q AND A

Q: *What types of foods are allowed with a nondiet approach?*

A: As you will see from the recipes in *The Smart Diet*, all foods are allowed in a healthful diet. Even desserts. This approach is about paying attention to the *quality* of foods eaten daily.

Include a variety of foods to keep meals interesting and to ensure that you get all the nutrients you need. As a guide, strive to meet the servings suggested by the USDA (for serving amounts see the Food Guide Pyramid at nal.usda.gov/fnic):

• 6 to 11 servings of breads, cereals, rice, and pastas

• 3 to 5 servings of vegetables

• 2 to 4 servings of fruit

• 2 to 3 servings of milk, yogurt, and cheese

• 2 to 3 servings of meat, poultry, fish, dry beans, eggs, and nuts

• Use fats and sweets sparingly

through what you're feeling, or check out some books on positive thinking. You'll probably discover that your body image was shaped by other people and outside influences. As an adult, you can refute those messages and use positive thoughts to shape your own body image.

Learn to care for yourself.

Get acquainted with your internal caretaker, the inner part of you that nurtures you, loves you unconditionally, and always treats you with kindness and respect. Listen carefully. Your internal caretaker gently coaxes you to eat when you're hungry and to stop when you're satisfied.

Respond to your small needs, such as putting on hand lotion when your hands feel dry, getting a drink of water when you're thirsty, or taking a moment for time alone, rather than waiting until you finish one more task. "A Dozen Little Luxuries for Self-Care" *(left)* is a starter list of small ways to treat yourself with love and respect.

Grow to love movement.

Whether you're a couch spud or an exercise fanatic, you'll do well to take an enlightened view of movement—for the joy of it. Look for new ways to fit activity into your daily life. Roll up the rug to dance to your favorite music, spend time strolling in the fresh air on your nearest walking path, play with your children or pet in the park, commune with nature as you weed your garden.

Shun the scale.

This is a tough one, especially if your day is made or ruined by what you weigh each morning. Most nondiet experts suggest not weighing yourself because it fuels a diet mentality and keeps you focused on a number rather than your value. If you choose to weigh in, do so only once a month on the same day on a reliable scale. While you're at it, ditch diet paraphernalia such as diet books or articles, calorie counters, food scales, and other contraptions that keep you in the diet mode.

Celebrate your size—now!

Human bodies are naturally diverse. We don't expect everyone to have the same height or hair color. All body sizes deserve appreciation and respect. Look at all the things you are—your interests, talents, accomplishments, and contributions—and celebrate how special you are. "A weight ideal means we all must be alike to be acceptable, and that just isn't true," says Woolsey. "We each should take pride in our uniqueness and realize self worth isn't based on a number on the scale."

Enlist support.

Surround yourself with positive, supportive family members and friends. Explain the nondiet approach and why it's important to you. Ask for their support and understanding. Tell weight critics that your size and shape are no longer up for discussion. Some of the websites listed in "Resources" (see *page 10*) offer online support.

Connect to your spiritual self.

Taking care of your spiritual needs is as important as tending to your physical, mental, and emotional needs. When you worry about food issues or have feelings of low self-esteem, the connection to your inner spirit can appear broken or muffled, but your

A DOZEN LITTLE LUXURIES FOR SELF-CARE

1. Buy yourself a luxurious new robe

2. Read a novel or one of your favorite magazines

3. Meditate or take a meditation class

4. Paint your toenails or give yourself a foot massage

5. Buy a new cookbook and treat yourself to a gourmet meal (Yes, it's OK!)

6. Take a nap in the middle of the day

7. Take the afternoon off and rent a favorite movie

8. Slip out of the office for a manicure

9. Treat yourself to some exquisite new undergarments

10. Meet a dear friend for cappuccino

11. Play with a child or a pet

12. Sit and do nothing

spirit is always present, waiting for you to reconnect. Journaling, meditation, yoga, prayer, solitude, and creative expressions, such as singing, dancing, painting, and writing poetry, are ways to get in touch with your inner spirit.

Start living your dream life today.

Live a full and exciting life now. Make a list of all the activities you've put on hold because you wanted to lose weight first. Pick the top one and do it now. Whether it's learning to tango, taking flying lessons, looking for a new job, or traveling to Italy, pursue your dreams—whatever you weigh.

GETTING FIT FOR THE FUN OF IT: A NEW VIEW OF EXERCISE

Here's a novel idea: Exercise can—and should—equal fun. This concept is not as alien as it seems. Think back to when you were a kid. Did you love to jump, skip, cartwheel, tumble, and run? Remember the sense of freedom and fun as you burst outside at recess to play in the fresh air?

That feeling of exuberance and exhilaration is how exercise—or body movement—is meant to feel. "Moving your body means returning to the joy of childhood play," says Dayle Hayes. "It means forgetting all the rules and shoulds about exercise and changing the concept from grueling workout to zestful playtime. Moving your body is one of the best ways to keep physical hunger signals on cue and to naturally lift sagging spirits."

THE BENEFITS OF EXERCISE

Whatever your weight, regular movement or activity can improve your fitness level, reduce your risk for chronic diseases, boost your energy level, and enhance your feelings of well-being. Health experts agree that you can reap benefits from as little as 30 minutes of moderate activity on most—and preferably all—days. You don't even have to get your daily 30 minutes all at one time. You can accumulate it in 10-minute chunks of activity throughout the day.

If you haven't been active for a while, start out slowly and check with your doctor first. For many people, taking a 10-minute walk after dinner a few nights a week is a good way to start. Even everyday activities such as mowing the lawn, washing windows, and vigorous housecleaning count toward the 30-minute total.

Your options for fun ways to include some type of movement are almost limitless. Structured activities such as aerobics classes and strength training are terrific, too, if that's what you enjoy. Weight training is especially beneficial for increasing muscle mass, which increases your metabolism (and translates to burning more calories). If you don't like classes, use exercise videos available for people of all fitness levels (check the website collagevideo.com for information on hundreds of exercise videos). When choosing physical activities, zero in on those that refresh a childlike sense of fun.

EATING FOR LIFE

Choosing a life without dieting will free you from your daily battle connected with food. It will also allow you to live life fully and more consciously. Food is meant to sustain you, but it also can bring you pleasure. Isn't it time to make peace with food?

Q AND A

Q: *Can I still be healthy if my weight falls in the overweight zone?*

A: Yes, you can be overweight and be in good health. "Research shows that larger people who are active and who eat a varied, nutritious diet can indeed be healthy," says Hayes. "Being fit and overweight sure beats being skinny and unfit." (See "I was thin but unfit," page 8.)

Just because a person is thin doesn't mean she is healthy. Although weight gain may not be your goal, accepting your optimal body size and weight should be.

If you're overweight, your weight might decrease once your eating normalizes. Losing and maintaining even a 5- or 10-pound weight loss can help reduce the risk for heart disease, diabetes, and some forms of cancer while alleviating health concerns, such as high blood pressure.

smartsna

cks

ratatouille pizza

This tomato, eggplant, and pepper pizza is an example of the healthful Mediterranean diet, with its abundance of vegetables and herbs.

½ cup chopped onion

2 cloves garlic, minced

1 tablespoon olive oil or cooking oil

4 medium tomatoes, peeled, seeded, and chopped

1 cup chopped, peeled eggplant

1 tablespoon snipped fresh thyme or 1 teaspoon dried thyme, crushed

½ teaspoon sugar

¼ teaspoon salt

⅛ teaspoon pepper

1 16-ounce thin-crust Italian bread shell (Boboli)

2 medium red and/or yellow tomatoes, halved lengthwise and sliced

1 small zucchini, sliced

1 small yellow summer squash, sliced

⅓ cup crumbled feta cheese

2 tablespoons sliced, pitted ripe olives

½ cup shredded mozzarella cheese

In a medium skillet cook onion and garlic in 2 teaspoons of the oil until tender. Add tomatoes, eggplant, thyme, sugar, salt, and pepper. Cook, uncovered, over medium-low heat about 15 minutes or until liquid is evaporated and mixture is of spreading consistency, stirring occasionally.

Place the bread shell on a lightly greased baking sheet. Spread the warm eggplant-tomato mixture onto bread shell. Arrange tomatoes, zucchini, and yellow summer squash on top. Brush vegetables with the remaining 1 teaspoon oil. Sprinkle with feta cheese and olives. Top with shredded mozzarella cheese.

Bake, uncovered, in a 400° oven for 12 to 15 minutes or until vegetables are warm and cheese is melted. Cut into wedges to serve. Makes 12 servings.

Nutrition Facts per serving: **166 cal.**, 6 g total fat (2 g sat. fat), 11 mg chol., 365 mg sodium, 22 g carbo., 2 g fiber, 7 g pro. ▶ Exchanges: 1½ Starch, 1 Vegetable, ½ Fat

Nutrition Facts per serving: 135 cal., 5 g total fat (2 g sat. fat), 11 mg chol., 262 mg sodium, 16 g carbo., 2 g fiber, 8 g pro. ▶ Exchanges: 1 Starch, ½ Vegetable, ½ Meat, ½ Fat

On a lightly floured surface divide dough into two portions. Cover; let dough rest for 10 minutes. Roll each dough portion into a 10- to 12-inch circle. Grease two extra-large baking sheets; sprinkle with cornmeal. Transfer dough circles to baking sheets. Bake in a 450° oven about 5 minutes. Remove baking sheets from oven; place on wire racks to cool.

Meanwhile, stir together olive oil and crushed red pepper; brush onto the crusts. Top with mozzarella cheese. Layer with the tomato slices and onion. Sprinkle basil and rosemary over tomatoes. Top with cheese. Bake for 5 to 8 minutes or until mozzarella cheese is melted and pizza crusts are golden brown. Cut each pizza into 8 wedges to serve. Makes 16 servings.

1 16-ounce **loaf frozen whole wheat bread dough, thawed**

2 tablespoons **cornmeal**

1 tablespoon **olive oil**

⅛ teaspoon **crushed red pepper**

1 cup **shredded reduced-fat mozzarella cheese**

6 **plum tomatoes, sliced**

1 small **red onion, cut into very thin wedges and separated into strips**

2 tablespoons **snipped fresh basil or oregano**

1 tablespoon **snipped fresh rosemary**

½ cup **shredded smoked Gouda cheese (2 ounces)**

smoky tomato pizza

Smoked Gouda and herbs add a sophisticated flair to this fresh tomato-topped appetizer pizza.

1 **16-ounce package hot roll mix**

⅓ **cup oil-packed dried tomatoes**

2 **3-ounce packages cream cheese, softened**

⅓ **cup finely chopped pitted ripe olives**

¼ **cup chopped green onions**

1 **slightly beaten egg yolk**

1 **teaspoon cracked black pepper**

2 **teaspoons fresh snipped oregano or thyme, or ½ teaspoon dried oregano or thyme, crushed (optional)**

1 **slightly beaten egg**

1 **tablespoon water**

Prepare the hot roll mix according to package directions. After kneading, divide the dough into two portions; cover and let rest for 5 minutes. Grease a large baking sheet; set aside.

For filling, drain tomatoes, reserving oil; chop the tomatoes. In a medium bowl combine tomatoes, cream cheese, olives, green onions, egg yolk, pepper, and, if desired, oregano or thyme. Stir in about 1 tablespoon of the reserved tomato oil, if necessary, to make a filling that is easy to spread.

Transfer dough portions to a lightly floured surface. Roll each portion to a 14×11-inch rectangle. Spread half of the filling over each rectangle to within ½ inch of edges (filling amount will seem generous). Roll up dough tightly from long sides; seal seams. Place loaves, seam sides down, on prepared baking sheet. Cover and let dough rise in a warm place until nearly double (about 30 to 40 minutes).

Using a sharp knife, make three or four diagonal cuts about ¼ inch deep in loaf tops. Combine egg and water; brush onto loaves. Bake in a 375° oven about 25 minutes or until golden. Carefully remove loaves from baking sheet; cool on wire racks. Serve warm or at room temperature. Makes 2 loaves (48 servings).

Although this loaf has no more calories than a slice of bread, it's studded with flavorful dried tomatoes, green onions, and olives.

herbed olive spirals

Nutrition Facts per serving: 67 cal., 1 g total fat (0 g sat. fat), 2 mg chol., 61 mg sodium, 11 g carbo., 1 g fiber, 3 g pro. ▶ Exchanges: ½ Starch, ½ Vegetable

2 large fresh poblano peppers

2 medium red sweet peppers

½ of an 8-ounce tub (½ cup) plain fat-free cream cheese

1 tablespoon snipped fresh cilantro

2 teaspoons lime juice

⅛ teaspoon ground red pepper

2 cloves garlic, minced

4 7-or 8-inch flour tortillas

To roast poblano and sweet peppers, halve peppers and remove stems, membranes, and seeds. Place peppers, cut sides down, on a baking sheet lined with foil. Bake peppers in a 425° oven for 20 to 25 minutes or until skin is bubbly and brown. Wrap the peppers in the foil; let stand for 15 to 20 minutes or until cool enough to handle. Using a paring knife, pull the skin off gently and slowly. Cut peppers into thin strips.

Meanwhile, stir together the cream cheese, cilantro, lime juice, ground red pepper, and garlic. Spread tortillas with cream cheese mixture. Lay poblano and sweet pepper strips over cream cheese mixture. Roll up tortillas. Wrap with clear plastic wrap; refrigerate up to 6 hours. Unwrap and bias-slice crosswise into 1¼-inch pieces. Makes 8 to 10 servings (about 24 slices).

These pinwheels of hot and sweet peppers are packed with flavor. Perfect for a party, the rolls can be made up to six hours in advance.

fiesta rolls

Combine luscious mangoes and kiwifruit for a dip that's all flavor and zero fat.

For dip, in a serving bowl combine mangoes, kiwifruit, sweet pepper, green onion, lime juice, cilantro, brown sugar, ginger, and ground red pepper. Toss to coat well. Cover and chill for up to 4 hours.

Meanwhile, for jicama chips use a sharp knife to peel and halve jicama; cut jicama into ¼-inch slices. Serve with dip. Makes eight ¼-cup servings.

Jicama Storage Tip: Jicama, a large tuberous root vegetable, is peeled before serving, just like a potato. Whole unpeeled jicamas can be stored in the refrigerator for up to 3 weeks. After peeling and cutting, wrap jicama tightly in plastic wrap and refrigerate for up to 1 week.

2 ripe mangoes, peeled, seeded, and finely chopped

1 kiwifruit, peeled and finely chopped

¼ cup finely chopped red sweet pepper

1 green onion, thinly sliced (2 tablespoons)

1 tablespoon lime juice

1 tablespoon snipped fresh cilantro, parsley, or basil

1 tablespoon brown sugar

1 teaspoon grated fresh ginger

Dash ground red pepper

1 medium jicama

Nutrition Facts per serving: 61 cal., 0 g total fat (0 g sat. fat), 0 mg chol., 2 mg sodium, 15 g carbo., 1 g fiber, 1 g pro. ▶ Exchanges: ½ Vegetable, ½ Fruit

marinated zucchini and mushrooms

Capture summer garden flavors in an appetizer that's marinated all day or overnight, whichever suits your schedule.

1 small **zucchini**

1 small **yellow summer squash**

1½ cups **small whole fresh mushrooms (4 ounces)**

½ of a small **red sweet pepper, cut into square pieces (½ cup)**

2 tablespoons **lemon juice**

1 tablespoon **olive oil**

1 teaspoon **sugar**

⅛ teaspoon **salt**

¾ teaspoon **snipped fresh tarragon or oregano, or** ⅛ **teaspoon dried tarragon or oregano, crushed**

⅛ teaspoon **black pepper**

1 clove **garlic, minced**

Fresh tarragon or oregano (optional)

Using a vegetable peeler, shave off long, thin strips of zucchini and yellow summer squash. In a plastic bag set in a large bowl place zucchini, summer squash, mushrooms, and sweet pepper.

For marinade, in small bowl stir together lemon juice, oil, sugar, salt, tarragon or oregano, pepper, and garlic. Pour marinade over vegetables in bag; seal bag. Marinate vegetables in the refrigerator for 8 hours or overnight, turning bag occasionally.

To serve, pour vegetables and marinade into a serving dish. If desired, garnish with fresh tarragon or oregano. Serve with toothpicks. Makes 6 to 8 servings.

Nutrition Facts per serving: 37 cal., 2 g total fat (0 g sat. fat), 0 mg chol., 47 mg sodium, 4 g carbo., 1 g fiber, 1 g pro. ▶ Exchanges: ½ Vegetable, ½ Fat

Nutrition Facts per serving: 77 cal., 3 g total fat (1 g sat. fat), 7 mg chol., 142 mg sodium, 10 g carbo., 1 g fiber, 4 g pro. ▶ Exchanges: ½ Starch, ½ Vegetable, ½ Fat

1 14-ounce can **artichoke hearts**, drained and finely chopped

3 **green onions**, thinly sliced

½ of an 8-ounce tub (½ cup) **light cream cheese**

⅓ cup **grated Parmesan cheese**

¼ cup **crumbled feta cheese**

3 tablespoons **reduced-fat pesto**

8 8-inch **flour tortillas**

1 8-ounce jar **roasted red sweet peppers**, drained and cut into strips

Nonstick cooking spray

1 8-ounce carton **plain yogurt** (optional)

1 tablespoon **snipped fresh chives** (optional)

For filling, in a large bowl stir together the artichoke hearts, green onions, cream cheese, Parmesan cheese, feta cheese, and pesto.

Spread about ¼ cup of the filling onto each tortilla. Top with roasted sweet pepper strips; roll up. Arrange tortillas in a greased 3-quart rectangular baking dish. Lightly spray rolls with nonstick cooking spray. Bake, uncovered, in a 350° oven about 15 minutes or until heated through.

Meanwhile, if desired, stir together the yogurt and chives. Cut each tortilla into thirds and arrange on a serving platter. If desired, serve with yogurt mixture. Makes 8 servings (24 pieces).

artichoke-feta tortilla wraps

Wrap three cheeses, roasted peppers, and artichokes in flour tortillas for this appetizer. For a colorful wrap, use red or green tortillas.

roasted eggplant spread

A food processor helps make this roasted vegetable spread a quick topping for bread slices.

Prick eggplant all over with a fork. Place on a rack in a roasting pan. Bake in a 375° oven for 40 minutes. Prick sweet pepper all over with a fork. Put pepper and onion on rack alongside eggplant. Bake about 30 minutes more or until all vegetables are very soft. Cool slightly.

Remove stems from eggplant and sweet pepper. Cut eggplant in half; scoop out as many seeds as possible. Chop eggplant coarsely and place in a food processor bowl. Cut sweet pepper in half; remove seeds and membranes. Peel skin from sweet pepper; add sweet pepper to processor bowl. Coarsely chop onion; add to processor bowl. Add capers, lemon juice, oil, and black pepper. Cover; process with a few on-and-off turns until mixture is slightly chunky but not smooth. Set aside.

Place bread slices on a baking sheet. Broil 3 to 4 inches from the heat about 1 minute or until lightly toasted; turn slices over and broil about 1 minute more or until lightly toasted. Top each slice with about 1 tablespoon eggplant mixture. If desired, cover and let stand for up to 1 hour before serving. If desired, sprinkle with parsley. Makes 16 servings.

1 small eggplant (about 10 ounces)

1 medium red sweet pepper

1 small onion, peeled

2 tablespoons capers, drained

2 teaspoons lemon juice

1 teaspoon olive oil

Dash black pepper

16 ½-inch slices Italian bread

Snipped fresh Italian parsley (optional)

Nutrition Facts per serving: 47 cal., 1 g total fat (0 g sat. fat), 0 mg chol., 96 mg sodium, 9 g carbo., 0 g fiber, 1 g pro. ▶ Exchanges: ½ Starch, ½ Vegetable

Nutrition Facts per serving: 32 cal., 1 g total fat (0 g sat. fat), 13 mg chol., 48 mg sodium, 3 g carbo., 0 g fiber, 2 g pro. ▶ Exchanges: ½ Starch

3 tablespoons olive oil

1 tablespoon lemon juice

1 tablespoon snipped fresh chives

1 tablespoon snipped fresh basil

1 tablespoon snipped fresh mint

1 teaspoon bottled minced garlic

6 ounces frozen crabmeat, thawed and drained, or one 6½-ounce can crabmeat, drained, flaked, and cartilage removed

8 ounces peeled, deveined, cooked shrimp, coarsely chopped

1 cup chopped plum tomatoes

½ cup finely chopped onion

1 8-ounce loaf baguette-style French bread

Freshly ground black pepper

Fresh mint (optional)

In a medium bowl stir together 1 tablespoon of the olive oil, lemon juice, chives, basil, mint, and garlic. Add crabmeat, shrimp, tomatoes, and onion; toss to coat. Cut the bread into 48 thin slices. Arrange bread slices on a large baking sheet. Brush one side of each slice with some of the remaining 2 tablespoons olive oil; sprinkle lightly with pepper.

Broil 3 to 4 inches from heat for 1 to 2 minutes or until toasted. Turn and broil other side until toasted.

To serve, spoon seafood mixture onto the oiled side of each slice. If desired, garnish with fresh mint. Serve immediately. Makes 48 servings.

Add class to the traditional tomato-and-herb-topped bruschetta with shrimp and crabmeat.

seafood bruschetta

curried crab dip

Yogurt cheese—made ahead of time—adds creaminess to this appetizer. Chutney and curry powder supply the Indian flavors.

Line a large strainer or yogurt sieve with a double thickness of 100-percent-cotton cheesecloth. Place strainer or a yogurt sieve over a medium bowl. Spoon yogurt into the strainer or sieve. Cover; refrigerate overnight. Discard any liquid in the bowl; wash and dry the bowl.

In the clean bowl combine drained yogurt, crabmeat, green onion, chutney, curry powder, salt, and red pepper. Cover and chill for up to 4 hours. If desired, garnish with additional green onion. Serve dip with crackers, carrots, or cucumbers. Makes 2 cups (sixteen 2-tablespoon servings).

2 8-ounce cartons plain fat-free yogurt (without gelatin)

1 cup cooked crabmeat (6 ounces)

1 green onion, thinly sliced

1 to 2 tablespoons chutney, snipped

1 teaspoon curry powder

¼ teaspoon salt

Dash ground red pepper

Thinly sliced green onion (optional)

Low-fat crackers, carrot sticks, and/or cucumber slices

DRINK TO YOUR HEALTH ▶ MIND·BODY·SPIRIT

Getting enough water will help prevent constipation and headaches and may help you lose weight. When you're dehydrated, your metabolism slows and you burn fewer calories. So, don't wait for a "thirsty" signal before you take a drink. At that point, you're already dehydrated. Shoot for all-day quaffing.

Nutrition Facts per 2 tablespoons plus 2 crackers: 41 cal., 0 g total fat (0 g sat. fat), 9 mg chol., 122 mg sodium, 5 g carbo., 0 g fiber, 4 g pro. ▶ Exchanges: 1 Fat

4 ounces crumbled feta cheese

½ of an 8-ounce package (½ cup) reduced-fat cream cheese (Neufchâtel), softened

⅓ cup light mayonnaise dressing or salad dressing

1 clove garlic, minced

¼ teaspoon dried basil, crushed, or 1 teaspoon snipped fresh basil

¼ teaspoon dried oregano, crushed, or 1 teaspoon snipped fresh oregano

⅛ teaspoon dried dillweed or ¾ teaspoon snipped fresh dill

⅛ teaspoon dried thyme, crushed, or ¾ teaspoon snipped fresh thyme

Assorted cut-up vegetables and crackers

In a food processor bowl or mixing bowl combine the feta cheese, cream cheese, mayonnaise dressing, garlic, basil, oregano, dill, and thyme. Cover and process or beat with an electric mixer on medium speed until combined.

Cover and chill spread until serving time. Serve with assorted vegetables and crackers. Makes 1½ cups (twelve 2-tablespoon servings).

Herb Storage Tip: Fresh herbs are perishable. It's best to purchase only as much as you need and use them fairly quickly. For short-term storage, with the exception of basil, wrap the stem ends in damp paper towels and place the herbs in the refrigerator. Place fresh basil stems in a container of about 2 inches of water. Do not refrigerate or the leaves will turn black.

Make this tangy spread early in the day so the flavors have time to blend. If you grow your own herbs, use them instead of the dried.

feta cheese spread

pita chips with red pepper dip

Roasted red peppers and fresh thyme create a big, bold flavor for crispy, baked pita chips.

To roast fresh peppers, cut into quarters lengthwise; remove seeds, membranes, and stems. Line a baking sheet with foil. Place the peppers, skin sides up, on baking sheet, pressing peppers to lie flat. Bake in a 425° oven about 20 minutes or until dark and blistered. Remove from oven and place in a clean paper bag. Close bag and let stand about 10 minutes. When cool enough to handle, peel the dark skins from peppers; discard skins.

Place roasted peppers in a blender container or food processor bowl. Cover; blend or process until finely chopped. Add tomato paste, sugar, thyme, salt, ground red pepper, and garlic. Cover; blend until nearly smooth. Serve with Baked Pita Chips. To store, cover and refrigerate dip for up to 1 week. Makes about ¾ cup (six 2-tablespoon servings).

Baked Pita Chips: Split 4 large pita bread rounds in half horizontally. Lightly spray the cut side of each pita bread half with nonstick cooking spray. Sprinkle each lightly with ½ to ¾ teaspoon onion or garlic powder or pepper. Cut each half into 6 wedges. Spread wedges in a single layer on a baking sheet. (You'll need to bake chips in batches.) Bake in a 350° oven for 10 to 12 minutes or until crisp. Serve with Red Pepper Dip. To store, place Baked Pita Chips in an airtight container for up to 1 week. Makes 48 chips.

2 medium red sweet peppers or one 7-ounce jar roasted red sweet peppers, drained

2 tablespoons tomato paste

1 teaspoon sugar

1 teaspoon snipped fresh thyme or ¼ teaspoon dried thyme, crushed

¼ teaspoon salt

Dash ground red pepper

1 clove garlic, minced, or ⅛ teaspoon garlic powder

1 recipe Baked Pita Chips

Nutrition Facts per 2 tablespoons and 4 chips: 74 cal., 0 g total fat (0 g sat. fat), 0 mg chol., 208 mg sodium, 15 g carbo., 1 g fiber, 3 g pro. ▶ Exchanges: ½ Starch, 1 Vegetable

Nutrition Facts per tablespoon: 124 cal., 6 g total fat (2 g sat. fat), 9 mg chol., 166 mg sodium, 14 g carbo., 1 g fiber, 4 g pro. ▶ Exchanges: ½ Starch, ½ Milk, ½ Fat

- 1 16-ounce carton plain low-fat yogurt (without gelatin)
- ¼ cup finely snipped dried apricots
- 1 tablespoon honey
- ¼ to ½ teaspoon coarsely ground black pepper
- ½ of an 8-ounce package (½ cup) reduced-fat cream cheese (Neufchâtel), softened
- 1 tablespoon finely chopped pistachio nuts
- Assorted crackers

Line a large strainer or yogurt sieve with a double thickness of 100-percent-cotton cheesecloth. Place strainer or sieve over a medium bowl. Stir together yogurt, apricots, honey, and pepper. Spoon mixture into strainer. Cover and refrigerate for 4 to 24 hours or until mixture is firm.

Discard any liquid in bowl; wash and dry bowl. Transfer yogurt mixture to clean bowl; stir in cream cheese. Sprinkle with nuts. Serve with assorted crackers. Makes 1½ cups (twelve 2-tablespoon servings).

peppercheese with apricots

Hot and sweet flavors—black pepper and apricots—commingle perfectly in this creamy yogurt cheese spread.

This is a spinach dip you can feel good about eating. Unlike most of its higher-fat cousins, this garlic-permeated dip is low in fat.

Peel away outer dry leaves from head of garlic, leaving skin of garlic cloves intact. Use a sharp knife to cut off pointed top portion of the garlic head (about ¼ inch), leaving the bulb intact. Place garlic head on a 12-inch square of a double thickness of foil. Drizzle garlic with the oil. Fold foil to enclose garlic. Bake in a 375° oven about 30 minutes or until garlic is soft. Cool.

Meanwhile, cook the spinach according to package directions. Drain well, pressing out excess liquid.

Squeeze garlic pulp from each clove into a food processor bowl, discarding skins. Add the cooked, drained spinach, milk, salt, and hot pepper sauce. Cover and process until combined. Add cream cheese. Cover and process until nearly smooth. Transfer spinach mixture to a saucepan. Cook and stir over medium-low heat until heated through.

To serve, transfer dip to a serving bowl. If desired, sprinkle with chopped tomato. Serve with Toasted Pita Wedges. Makes eight ¼-cup servings.

Toasted Pita Wedges: Split 8 small pita bread rounds in half horizontally; cut each half into 6 wedges. Place wedges, cut sides up, on an ungreased baking sheet. Bake in a 375° oven for 7 to 9 minutes or until light brown. Store leftover wedges in an airtight container.

1 medium whole head garlic

1 teaspoon olive oil

1 10-ounce package frozen chopped spinach

¼ cup fat-free milk

⅛ teaspoon salt

Dash bottled hot pepper sauce

1 8-ounce package reduced-fat cream cheese (Neufchâtel), cut up

Chopped tomato (optional)

1 recipe Toasted Pita Wedges

Nutrition Facts per ¼ cup dip and 6 wedges: 133 cal., 7 g total fat (4 g sat. fat), 22 mg chol., 246 mg sodium, 12 g carbo., 0 g fiber, 5 g pro. ▶ Exchanges: ½ Starch, 1 Vegetable, 1 Fat

CHAPTER TWO

betterbrea

kfasts

Nutrition Facts per serving: 251 cal., 14 g total fat (2 g sat. fat), 223 mg chol., 770 mg sodium, 16 g carbo., 1 g fiber, 18 g pro. ▶ Exchanges: 2 Vegetable, 2 Meat, 2 Fat

2 teaspoons **olive oil**

¼ cup **chopped onion**

1 cup **sliced fresh mushrooms**

2 cloves **garlic, minced**

¼ teaspoon **dried thyme, crushed, or 1 teaspoon snipped fresh thyme**

1 8-ounce can **stewed tomatoes, drained**

2 **eggs plus 2 large egg whites or 1 cup refrigerated or frozen egg product, thawed**

2 tablespoons **water**

¼ teaspoon **black pepper**

⅛ teaspoon **salt**

Nonstick cooking spray

¼ cup **finely shredded Asiago cheese**

In a small skillet heat 1 teaspoon of the oil over medium heat. Add onion; cook and stir for 3 minutes. Add the mushrooms, garlic, and (if using dried rather than fresh) the dried thyme; cook and stir for 3 minutes more. Add the tomatoes. Simmer, uncovered, for 5 minutes.

Meanwhile, in a medium bowl beat together eggs and egg whites or egg product, water, pepper, and salt. Lightly coat a 10-inch nonstick skillet with flared sides with nonstick cooking spray. Heat skillet over medium heat until hot. Add remaining 1 teaspoon olive oil, swirling to coat pan. Add egg mixture to hot skillet. Cook for 3 to 4 minutes or until bottom of omelet is set (top will be wet); gently lift edges with a spatula to allow liquid to run under omelet.

Spoon half of tomato mixture over one side of the omelet; sprinkle with some of the cheese and (if using fresh rather than dried) the fresh thyme. Using a wide spatula, fold omelet in half. Cut omelet in half; transfer to 2 serving plates. Spoon remaining tomato mixture over each omelet. Top with remaining cheese. Makes 2 servings.

This pillow of eggs—enfolding a mushroom, tomato, and cheese filling— is ready in about 20 minutes. Serve with toasted English muffins.

provençale omelet

chorizo frittata

Chorizo is so well-seasoned that a little goes a long way to flavor this robust red pepper-potato frittata.

Lightly coat a medium skillet with nonstick cooking spray; add potato to skillet. Cook potato, covered, over medium heat about 5 minutes or until lightly browned and just tender, turning occasionally. Add sausage, sweet pepper, and green onion. Cook for 2 to 3 minutes, covered, or until sausage is heated through and vegetables are tender. Remove from heat. Arrange potato and other ingredients so they are evenly distributed over bottom of skillet.

Combine eggs, egg whites, milk, oregano, salt, and, if desired, black pepper. Pour over vegetable mixture in skillet; do not stir. Place skillet over medium heat. As mixture sets, run a spatula around edge of skillet, lifting edge with the spatula to allow liquid to run under frittata. Continue cooking and lifting edges until egg mixture is set (top will be wet). Remove from heat; let stand, covered, for 5 minutes. Loosen edges; transfer to a serving plate. To serve, cut into wedges. Makes 2 servings.

Nonstick cooking spray

½ cup chopped potato

¼ cup finely chopped cooked chorizo or other spicy cooked sausage

¼ cup finely chopped red sweet pepper

2 tablespoons sliced green onion

3 eggs

3 egg whites

2 tablespoons fat-free milk

1 teaspoon snipped fresh oregano or ½ teaspoon dried oregano, crushed

⅛ teaspoon salt

⅛ teaspoon black pepper (optional)

Nutrition Facts per serving: 188 cal., 16 g total fat (5 g sat. fat), 320 mg chol., 322 mg sodium, 12 g carbo., 1 g fiber, 21 g pro. ▶ Exchanges: 1 Starch, 2½ Meat, 1 Fat

Nutrition Facts per serving: 114 cal., 5 g total fat (2 g sat. fat), 58 mg chol., 164 mg sodium, 6 g carbo., 1 g fiber, 11 g pro. ▶ Exchanges: 1 Vegetable, 1½ Meat, 1 Fat

1 small zucchini, halved lengthwise and thinly sliced

½ cup chopped red onion

½ cup chopped red or green sweet pepper

2 cloves garlic, minced

2 teaspoons olive oil or cooking oil

6 egg whites

1 egg

1 cup fat-free milk

1 tablespoon shredded fresh basil

¼ cup shredded mozzarella cheese (1 ounce)

Chopped tomato (optional)

In a medium skillet cook zucchini, onion, sweet pepper, and garlic in hot oil until onion is tender. Set aside.

In a medium bowl stir together the egg whites, egg, milk, and basil. Stir in zucchini mixture. Pour into 4 individual quiche dishes or shallow casseroles, about 4½ inches in diameter.

Bake in a 350° oven for 15 to 20 minutes or until set. Sprinkle each serving with mozzarella cheese. Let stand for 5 minutes before serving. If desired, sprinkle with chopped tomato. Makes 4 servings.

Garlic Storage Tip: Keep garlic on hand for adding a boost of flavor to many recipes—without adding fat or calories. Store fresh garlic in a cool, dry, dark place. Leave the bulb whole, as individual cloves dry out quickly. Minced garlic is available in easy-to-use jars and will keep in the refrigerator for up to 6 months.

Individual crustless quiches—with zucchini, garlic, basil, and mozzarella—give a weekend brunch panache.

italian baked eggs

Nutrition Facts per serving: 258 cal., 10 g total fat (2 g sat. fat), 5 mg chol., 491 mg sodium, 15 g carbo., 0 g fiber, 25 g pro. ▶ Exchanges: 1 Starch, 3 Meat, 1 Fat

1 tablespoon margarine or butter

3 8-ounce cartons refrigerated or frozen egg product, thawed

1 cup fat-free milk

½ cup all-purpose flour

2 tablespoons grated Parmesan cheese

Nonstick cooking spray

2 tablespoons snipped fresh basil or parsley or 2 teaspoons dried basil or parsley, crushed

¾ teaspoon snipped fresh thyme or ¼ teaspoon dried thyme, crushed

⅛ teaspoon salt

Dash pepper

For puff, place margarine or butter in a 10-inch ovenproof nonstick skillet. Place skillet in a 400° oven for 3 to 5 minutes or until margarine melts. Meanwhile, in a medium bowl combine ¾ cup of the egg product, ½ cup of the milk, flour, and Parmesan cheese; beat until smooth. Tilt skillet to coat with melted margarine or butter. Immediately pour egg product mixture into the hot skillet. Return to oven and bake about 25 minutes or until puffed and brown.

Meanwhile, for eggs, lightly coat a large skillet with nonstick cooking spray. Heat skillet over medium heat until hot. In a medium bowl combine remaining egg product, remaining milk, basil or parsley, thyme, salt, and pepper; pour into skillet. Cook over medium heat, without stirring, until mixture begins to set on the bottom and around the edge.

Using a large spoon or spatula, lift and fold partially cooked egg mixture so uncooked portion flows underneath. Continue cooking over medium heat for 3 to 4 minutes or until eggs are cooked through but are still glossy and moist. To serve, immediately spoon egg mixture into puff; cut into wedges. Makes 4 servings.

Bake a puff in one ovenproof skillet, scramble eggs in another skillet, and combine them for an extraordinary breakfast entrée.

puffed egg scramble

Wild mushrooms and smoked chicken supply the flavor for the rich, creamy sauce used in this baked egg dish.

smoked chicken egg bake

For sauce, in a screw-top jar combine milk and flour. Cover; shake well to combine. Pour into a saucepan; cook and stir over medium heat until bubbly. Add cream cheese; cook and stir until melted. Remove from heat; stir in chives.

Lightly coat a large skillet with nonstick cooking spray. Heat skillet over medium-high heat until hot. Add mushrooms and onion. Cook and stir about 3 minutes or until tender. Add mushroom mixture and chicken to sauce; set aside.

In the same skillet melt margarine or butter. Add egg product, salt, and pepper. Cook over medium heat without stirring until egg mixture begins to set around edges. Using a large spatula, lift and fold the partially cooked egg mixture so uncooked portion flows underneath. Continue cooking until eggs are cooked throughout but are still moist. Transfer mixture to a 2-quart casserole; spoon sauce over top. Bake, uncovered, in a 400° oven about 15 minutes or until heated through. Let stand for 10 minutes before serving. Makes 6 servings.

1¼ cups fat-free milk

2 tablespoons all-purpose flour

2 ounces reduced-fat cream cheese (Neufchâtel), cubed

2 tablespoons snipped fresh chives

Nonstick cooking spray

1½ cups sliced fresh wild mushrooms (such as morel or shiitake)

¼ cup chopped onion

1½ cups coarsely chopped smoked cooked chicken

1 tablespoon margarine or butter

2½ cups refrigerated or frozen egg product, thawed

¼ teaspoon salt

⅛ teaspoon black pepper

Nutrition Facts per serving: 263 cal., 15 g total fat (5 g sat. fat), 37 mg chol., 626 mg sodium, 9 g carbo., 0 g fiber, 23 g pro. ▶ Exchanges: 1 Vegetable, 3 Meat, 2 Fat

shrimp-artichoke frittata

A frittata makes a great breakfast or brunch food.
For a real treat, make it for dinner during the week.

Thaw shrimp, if frozen. Peel and devein shrimp. Rinse shrimp; pat dry. Halve shrimp lengthwise; set aside. Meanwhile, cook artichoke hearts according to package directions; drain. Cut artichoke hearts in quarters; set aside.

Stir together egg product, milk, green onions, garlic powder, and pepper; set aside.

Lightly coat a large nonstick skillet with nonstick cooking spray. Heat skillet until a drop of water sizzles. Add shrimp to skillet; cook shrimp for 1 to 3 minutes or until shrimp turn opaque.

Pour egg mixture into skillet; do not stir. Place skillet over medium-low heat. As the egg mixture sets, run a spatula around the edge of the skillet, lifting edges to allow liquid to run underneath. Continue cooking and lifting edges until mixture is almost set (top will be wet).

Remove skillet from heat; sprinkle artichoke pieces evenly over the top. Sprinkle with Parmesan cheese. Let stand, covered, for 3 to 4 minutes or until top is set. Loosen edges of frittata. Transfer to a serving plate; cut into wedges to serve. If desired, garnish with cherry tomatoes and parsley. Makes 4 servings.

4 ounces fresh or frozen shrimp in shells

½ of a 9-ounce package frozen artichoke hearts

2 cups refrigerated or frozen egg product, thawed

¼ cup fat-free milk

¼ cup thinly sliced green onions

⅛ teaspoon garlic powder

⅛ teaspoon pepper

Nonstick cooking spray

3 tablespoons finely shredded Parmesan cheese

Cherry tomatoes, quartered (optional)

Italian parsley (optional)

Nutrition Facts per serving: 126 cal., 3 g total fat (1 g sat. fat), 37 mg chol., 343 mg sodium, 6 g carbo., 2 g fiber, 19 g pro. ▶ Exchanges: ½ Vegetable, 2½ Meat

½ pound whole, tiny new potatoes, cut into ¼-inch slices

1 cup asparagus, cut into ½-inch pieces

Nonstick cooking spray

1½ cups refrigerated or frozen egg product, thawed

1 tablespoon snipped fresh parsley

1 teaspoon snipped fresh rosemary

¼ to ½ teaspoon onion powder

¼ teaspoon salt

¼ teaspoon pepper

1 large tomato, seeded and coarsely chopped

1 tablespoon finely shredded Parmesan cheese

In a large nonstick skillet cook potatoes in a small amount of boiling water, covered, for 5 minutes. Add asparagus; cover and cook for 5 to 7 minutes more or until vegetables are tender. Remove from skillet; drain well. Cool and dry the skillet. Lightly coat the skillet with nonstick cooking spray. Return vegetables to skillet.

In a medium bowl combine egg product, parsley, rosemary, onion powder, salt, and pepper. Pour over vegetables in skillet; do not stir. Place skillet over medium heat. As mixture sets, run a spatula around the edge of the skillet, lifting edges with the spatula to allow liquid to run underneath. Continue cooking and lifting edges until the egg mixture is almost set (top will be wet).

Remove skillet from heat; let stand, covered, for 3 to 4 minutes or until top is set. Top with chopped tomato and sprinkle with Parmesan cheese. Makes 4 servings.

One skillet and the freshest ingredients make for a satisfying meal modeled after European bistro fare.

asparagus and potato skillet

country-style turkey sausage

Select a skinless turkey breast and have the meat department grind it for you so you'll know it's 100 percent white meat.

Lightly coat a large skillet with nonstick cooking spray; set aside. In a medium bowl combine egg white, onion, apples, oats, parsley, salt, sage, nutmeg, black pepper, and red pepper. Add turkey; mix well. Shape mixture into eight 2-inch-diameter patties.

Heat skillet over medium heat; add patties to skillet. Cook patties for 10 to 12 minutes or until meat is no longer pink and juices run clear, turning once. Drain off fat. Makes 8 servings.

Nonstick cooking spray

1 slightly beaten egg white

¼ cup finely chopped onion

¼ cup finely snipped dried apples or ½ cup finely chopped fresh apple

3 tablespoons quick-cooking rolled oats

2 tablespoons snipped fresh parsley

½ teaspoon salt

½ teaspoon ground sage

¼ teaspoon ground nutmeg

¼ teaspoon black pepper

Dash ground red pepper

8 ounces ground raw white turkey meat

MIND·BODY·SPIRIT ▶ LEARNING FOR LIFE

How can you live to be 100? Having good genes helps, but scientists are finding that people who live a long time tend to make their lives worth living. Education and the desire to keep learning throughout life are keys to longevity. Take a class, learn how to play chess, or fill out a crossword puzzle. It may give you long life.

Nutrition Facts per serving: 49 cal., 1 g total fat (0 g sat. fat), 12 mg chol., 155 mg sodium, 4 g carbo., 0 g fiber, 6 g pro. ▶ Exchanges: 1 Meat

lemon breakfast parfaits

Serve these lively, layered parfaits of fruit and couscous for a smart start in the morning.

¾ cup **fat-free milk**

Dash **salt**

⅓ cup **couscous**

½ cup **lemon low-fat yogurt**

½ cup **reduced-calorie dairy sour cream**

1 tablespoon **honey**

¼ teaspoon **finely shredded lemon peel**

3 cups **assorted fruit, such as sliced strawberries, kiwifruit, nectarine, or star fruit; and/or blueberries or raspberries**

Chopped crystallized ginger (optional)

Fresh mint (optional)

In a medium saucepan bring the milk and salt to boiling; stir in the couscous. Simmer, covered, for 1 minute. Remove from heat; let stand for 5 minutes. Stir with a fork until fluffy. Cool.

In a small bowl combine the yogurt, sour cream, honey, and lemon peel; stir into the couscous. In another bowl combine desired fruit.

To serve, divide half of the fruit mixture among 6 parfait glasses. Spoon couscous mixture over fruit; top with remaining fruit. If desired, garnish with chopped crystallized ginger and mint. Makes 6 servings.

Nutrition Facts per serving: 127 cal., 2 g total fat (1 g sat. fat), 6 mg chol., 70 mg sodium, 22 g carbo., 2 g fiber, 5 g pro. ▶ Exchanges: 1 Starch, ½ Fruit, ½ Fat

Nutrition Facts per slice: 150 cal., 1 g total fat (0 g sat. fat), 30 mg chol., 163 mg sodium, 29 g carbo., 0 g fiber, 7 g pro. ▶ Exchanges: 1½ Starch, ½ Fruit, ½ Meat

½ cup **fat-free cream cheese** (about 5 ounces)

2 tablespoons **apricot or strawberry spreadable fruit**

8 **1-inch slices French bread**

2 **slightly beaten egg whites**

1 **beaten egg**

¾ cup **fat-free milk**

½ teaspoon **vanilla**

⅛ teaspoon **apple pie spice**

Nonstick cooking spray

½ cup **apricot or strawberry spreadable fruit**

In a small bowl stir together cream cheese and the 2 tablespoons spreadable fruit. Using a serrated knife, form a pocket in each of the bread slices by making a cut in the top crust almost to the bottom crust. Fill each pocket with some of the cream cheese mixture.

In a shallow bowl beat together the egg whites, egg, milk, vanilla, and apple pie spice. Lightly coat a nonstick griddle with nonstick cooking spray. Preheat over medium heat.

Dip stuffed bread slices into egg white mixture, coating both sides. Place bread slices on hot griddle; cook about 3 minutes or until golden brown, turning once.

Meanwhile, in a small saucepan heat the ½ cup spreadable fruit until melted, stirring frequently. Serve over French toast. Makes 8 slices.

French toast stuffed with apricot spread and cream cheese revs up sleepy palates.

stuffed french toast

honey-apple pancakes

These pancakes are like breakfast apple pies—a well-deserved weekend treat.

In a medium bowl stir together flour, baking powder, salt, apple pie spice, and baking soda. Make a well in the center of the flour mixture; set aside. In a small bowl stir together egg, apple juice, honey, and oil. Add egg mixture all at once to flour mixture, stirring until mixed but still slightly lumpy.

Lightly coat a nonstick griddle or heavy skillet with nonstick cooking spray. Heat over medium heat. For each pancake, pour about ¼ cup of the batter onto the hot griddle or skillet. Cook for 2 to 3 minutes or until pancakes have bubbly surfaces and edges are slightly dry. Turn pancakes; cook for 2 to 3 minutes more or until golden brown. Makes eight 4-inch pancakes.

1¼ cups all-purpose flour

2 teaspoons baking powder

¼ teaspoon salt

¼ teaspoon apple pie spice

⅛ teaspoon baking soda

1 beaten egg

¾ cup apple juice

2 tablespoons honey

1 tablespoon cooking oil

Nonstick cooking spray

Nutrition Facts per pancake: 236 cal., 5 g total fat (1 g sat. fat), 53 mg chol., 372 mg sodium, 42 g carbo., 1 g fiber, 5 g pro. ▶ Exchanges: 2½ Starch, 1 Fat

Nutrition Facts per serving: 117 cal., 0 g total fat (0 g sat. fat), 2 mg chol., 78 mg sodium, 24 g carbo., 1 g fiber, 6 g pro. ▶ Exchanges: ½ Fruit, ½ Milk

½ of a medium papaya, peeled, seeded, and chopped (¾ cup)

½ cup fresh strawberries

½ cup fat-free milk

½ cup plain fat-free yogurt

1 tablespoon honey

3 large ice cubes or ⅓ cup crushed ice

Papaya or strawberry slices (optional)

Fresh mint (optional)

In a blender container combine papaya, strawberries, milk, yogurt, and honey. Cover and blend until smooth.

With the blender running, add ice cubes, one at a time, through the opening in the lid. Pour into 2 tall glasses. If desired, garnish with papaya or strawberry and mint. Serve immediately. Makes 2 servings.

Papaya Tips: Choose papayas that are partially yellow and feel slightly soft when pressed. The skin should be smooth and free from bruises or very soft spots. A firm, unripe papaya can be ripened at room temperature for 3 to 5 days until mostly yellow to yellowish orange in color. Store a ripe papaya in a paper or plastic bag in the refrigerator for up to 1 week.

Breakfast doesn't have to be labor-intensive. This tasty shake is as easy as it is healthful.

strawberry-papaya shake

baked breakfast apples

Skipping breakfast can put your metabolism into slow gear. Start the day off right with a warm apple compote.

In two individual casseroles combine apples and dates. Sprinkle with cinnamon. Pour half the apple juice over each apple mixture. Bake, covered, in a 350° oven for 20 to 25 minutes or until apples are slightly tender. Stir spreadable fruit; spoon over apple mixtures. Sprinkle with granola. Serve warm. Makes 2 servings.

Microwave Directions: In two individual microwave-safe casseroles combine the apple and dates. Sprinkle with the cinnamon. Reduce apple juice to ¼ cup; divide evenly between casseroles. Microwave, covered, on 100 percent power (high) for 3 to 4 minutes or until apples are slightly tender. Stir spreadable fruit; spoon over apple mixture. Sprinkle with granola. Serve warm.

2 medium apples, cut into bite-size pieces

2 tablespoons snipped, pitted dates

¼ teaspoon ground cinnamon

½ cup apple juice

1 tablespoon raspberry spreadable fruit

¼ cup low-fat granola

TAKE TWO LAUGHS ▶ MIND·BODY·SPIRIT

A good belly laugh can improve your emotional and physical health, according to medical experts. Next time you're in a traffic jam, try thinking of a joke or something amusing instead of leaning on the horn. You'll reduce your anxiety and stress levels, which can take huge tolls on your immune system.

Nutrition Facts per serving: **188** cal., 1 g total fat (0 g sat. fat), 0 mg chol., 15 mg sodium, 47 g carbo., 4 g fiber, 1 g pro. ▶ Exchanges: ½ Starch, 2 Fruit

Nutrition Facts per serving: 203 cal., 5 g total fat (1 g sat. fat), 0 mg chol., 207 mg sodium, 37 g carbo., 2 g fiber, 3 g pro. ▶ Exchanges: 1½ Starch, ½ Fruit, 1 Fat

Nonstick cooking spray

⅔ cup all-purpose flour

½ cup whole wheat flour

1 teaspoon baking soda

1 teaspoon ground cinnamon

¼ teaspoon salt

1½ cups finely chopped, peeled apples

¼ cup refrigerated or frozen egg product, thawed

¾ cup sugar

¼ cup chopped walnuts or pecans

¼ cup applesauce

1 recipe Crumb Topping

Lightly coat a 9×1½-inch round baking pan with nonstick cooking spray; set aside. In a small bowl combine all-purpose flour, whole wheat flour, baking soda, cinnamon, and salt; set aside. In a large bowl toss together the apple and egg product. Stir in the sugar, walnuts, and applesauce. Add flour mixture; stir just until combined. Pour batter into the prepared pan. Sprinkle Crumb Topping over batter.

Bake in a 350° oven for 30 to 35 minutes or until a toothpick inserted near the center comes out clean. Cool coffeecake in pan about 10 minutes. Serve warm. Makes 10 servings.

Crumb Topping: In a small bowl stir together ¼ cup packed brown sugar, 1 tablespoon all-purpose flour, 1 tablespoon whole wheat flour, and ½ teaspoon ground cinnamon; cut in 1 tablespoon butter until crumbly. Stir in ¼ cup chopped walnuts or pecans.

Applesauce is the secret ingredient that lets you leave out the fat while creating a moist coffee cake.

apple coffee cake

herb-bran muffins

Partner these custom muffins (you choose the herb) with a frittata or omelet.

Nonstick cooking spray

1½ cups all-purpose flour

1 cup whole bran cereal

2 tablespoons grated Parmesan cheese

1 tablespoon sugar

½ teaspoon baking powder

¼ teaspoon baking soda

2 teaspoons snipped fresh basil, dill, rosemary, thyme, sage, or chives

2 beaten egg whites or 1 beaten egg

1 cup buttermilk

¼ cup cooking oil

Lightly coat ten to twelve 2½-inch muffin cups with nonstick cooking spray; set aside. In a large bowl stir together the flour, cereal, Parmesan cheese, sugar, baking powder, baking soda, and desired herb. Make a well in the center of the flour mixture.

In a small bowl combine egg whites or egg, buttermilk, and cooking oil. Add all at once to flour mixture. Stir just until moistened (batter will be lumpy).

Spoon batter into muffin cups. Bake in a 400° oven about 20 minutes or until golden. Cool on a wire rack about 5 minutes. Remove muffins from pan; serve warm. Makes 10 to 12 muffins.

Nutrition Facts per muffin: 162 cal., 7 g total fat (1 g sat. fat), 23 mg chol., 200 mg sodium, 22 g carbo., 3 g fiber, 5 g pro. ▶ Exchanges: 2 Starch, 1 Fat

Nutrition Facts per muffin: 155 cal., 5 g total fat (1 g sat. fat), 2 mg chol., 131 mg sodium, 27 g carbo., 2 g fiber, 5 g pro. ▶ Exchanges: 1½ Starch, 1 Fat

Nonstick cooking spray

1¼ cups **all-purpose flour**

¾ cup **packed brown sugar**

1 tablespoon **baking powder**

½ teaspoon **ground ginger**

¼ teaspoon **salt**

1 cup **chopped, peeled pears**

1 cup **whole bran cereal**

1 cup **skim milk**

¼ cup **refrigerated or frozen egg product, thawed**

¼ cup **cooking oil**

2 tablespoons **finely chopped almonds**

1 recipe **Ginger-Cream Spread**

Lightly coat 14 to 16 muffin cups with cooking spray or line with paper bake cups; set aside. In a large bowl stir together flour, brown sugar, baking powder, ginger, and salt. Add pears, stirring to coat. In a medium bowl stir together the cereal and milk; let cereal mixture stand for 5 minutes. Stir in egg product and oil; add to the pear mixture, stirring just until moistened. (If desired, cover and refrigerate the batter in an airtight container for up to 3 days. Bake as many muffins as needed.)

Spoon batter into prepared cups, filling each three-quarters full. Sprinkle with nuts. Bake in a 400° oven for 18 to 20 minutes or until a toothpick inserted near the centers comes out clean. Cool on a wire rack about 5 minutes. Remove from cups. Serve warm with Ginger-Cream Spread. Makes 14 to 16 muffins.

Ginger-Cream Spread: In a small bowl stir together ⅔ of an 8-ounce tub fat-free cream cheese, 1 tablespoon honey, and 1 tablespoon finely chopped crystallized ginger or ¼ teaspoon ground ginger until combined.

Ginger- and honey-laced cream cheese complements these pear-packed muffins. They're great for breakfast or for a midmorning snack.

pear-almond muffins

blueberry breakfast scones

Nothing is finer in the morning than these warm, blueberry-studded scones drizzled with a sweet orange glaze.

2 cups all-purpose flour

¼ cup sugar

1 tablespoon baking powder

1 tablespoon finely shredded orange peel

¼ teaspoon salt

¼ teaspoon baking soda

¼ cup margarine or butter

½ cup buttermilk or sour fat-free milk

¼ cup refrigerated or frozen egg product, thawed

1 teaspoon vanilla

1 cup fresh or frozen blueberries

1 recipe Orange Powdered Sugar Icing

Lightly grease a baking sheet; set aside. In a large bowl stir together flour, sugar, baking powder, orange peel, salt, and baking soda. Cut in margarine until mixture resembles coarse crumbs. Make a well in center of flour mixture. Stir together buttermilk, egg product, and vanilla; add to flour mixture all at once. Stir with a fork just until moistened. Gently stir in blueberries.

Transfer the dough to a lightly floured surface. Quickly knead dough by folding and pressing gently for 12 to 15 strokes or until dough is nearly smooth. Pat dough into a 7-inch circle on prepared baking sheet. Cut dough into 10 wedges.

Bake in a 400° oven for 15 to 20 minutes or until golden. Remove from the baking sheet; let cool on a wire rack while preparing icing. Drizzle Orange Powdered Sugar Icing over tops of scones. Serve warm. Makes 10 scones.

Orange Powdered Sugar Icing: In a small bowl stir together ¾ cup sifted powdered sugar and ¼ teaspoon finely shredded orange peel in a small bowl. Add enough orange juice or fat-free milk (3 to 4 teaspoons) to make of drizzling consistency.

Nutrition Facts per scone: 194 cal., 5 g total fat (1 g sat. fat), 1 mg chol., 273 mg sodium, 34 g carbo., 1 g fiber, 4 g pro. ▶ Exchanges: 2 Starch, 1 Fat

Nutrition Facts per serving: 211 cal., 7 g total fat (1 g sat. fat), 27 mg chol., 177 mg sodium, 34 g carbo., 1 g fiber, 4 g pro. ▶ Exchanges: 2 Starch, 1 Fat

1¼ cups **all-purpose flour**

½ cup **granulated sugar**

½ teaspoon **baking powder**

½ teaspoon **baking soda**

¾ teaspoon **ground cinnamon**

⅛ teaspoon **salt**

1 **beaten egg**

⅔ cup **buttermilk**

3 tablespoons **cooking oil**

½ teaspoon **vanilla**

1 cup **fresh or frozen raspberries**

2 tablespoons **brown sugar**

1 tablespoon **all-purpose flour**

2 teaspoons **butter or margarine**

Sifted powdered sugar

Lightly grease and flour a 9×1½-inch round baking pan; set aside. In a large bowl stir together the 1¼ cups flour, granulated sugar, baking powder, baking soda, ½ teaspoon of the cinnamon, and salt. In a small bowl stir together egg, buttermilk, oil, and vanilla. Add egg mixture to flour mixture. Stir with a fork just until moistened. Pour batter into prepared pan. Sprinkle raspberries over batter.

In a small bowl combine brown sugar, the 1 tablespoon flour, and the remaining ¼ teaspoon cinnamon. Cut in butter or margarine until mixture resembles coarse crumbs. Sprinkle over top of berries.

Bake in a 350° oven for 30 to 35 minutes or until a toothpick inserted near the center comes out clean. Cool in pan about 10 minutes on a wire rack. Remove coffee cake from pan; cool slightly. Sprinkle with powdered sugar. Serve warm. Makes 8 servings.

raspberry coffee cake

Imagine your favorite coffee cake topped with red raspberries and crumb topping. You won't want to skip breakfast.

cinnamon-pecan ring

This coffee cake is made the night before and baked in the morning.
Timesaving frozen bread dough is the star ingredient.

Grease a 12-inch pizza pan; set aside. Flatten thawed dough slightly on a lightly floured surface. Cut each loaf into four pieces. Form each piece into a rope about 18 inches long. Brush each rope lightly on all sides with melted margarine or butter.

Stir together granulated sugar, brown sugar, and cinnamon; place in a shallow pan or on a large sheet of foil. Roll one dough rope in sugar mixture to coat evenly. Shape rope into a coil in the center of the prepared pizza pan. Roll another rope in sugar. Attach securely to end of first rope; coil around first coil. Continue coating ropes with sugar and attaching to form a 10- to 11-inch circle. Sprinkle any remaining sugar mixture over coil. Sprinkle the pecans on top.

Cover with plastic wrap; let rise overnight in refrigerator. Remove from refrigerator; let stand for 15 to 20 minutes before baking. (Or, cover and let rise in a warm place for 30 to 40 minutes or until nearly double.) Bake in a 350° oven for 30 to 35 minutes or until done. Cover with foil for the last 10 minutes, if necessary, to prevent overbrowning. Cool about 15 minutes. Transfer to a serving plate. Drizzle with Powdered Sugar Icing. Serve warm. Makes 16 servings.

Powdered Sugar Icing: In a small bowl stir together 1¼ cups sifted powdered sugar and ½ teaspoon vanilla. Add enough milk (about 4 teaspoons) to make of drizzling consistency.

2 16-ounce loaves frozen bread dough, thawed

¼ cup margarine or butter, melted

⅓ cup granulated sugar

⅓ cup packed brown sugar

2 teaspoons ground cinnamon

½ cup chopped pecans

1 recipe Powdered Sugar Icing

Nutrition Facts per serving: 257 cal., 9 g total fat (1 g sat. fat), 0 mg chol., 280 mg sodium, 43 g carbo., 7 g fiber, 6 g pro. ▶ Exchanges: 2½ Starch, 1 Fat

wise entré

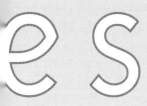

e s

apple-glazed chicken with spinach

Apple jelly is the secret ingredient that replaces fat for basting the chicken and flavors the spinach. Wild rice makes a perfect side dish.

For glaze, in a small saucepan heat the apple jelly, soy sauce, thyme, lemon peel, and ginger just until jelly is melted. Reserve ¼ cup of the glaze.

Place the chicken on the unheated rack of a broiler pan. Broil 5 to 6 inches from the heat for 10 to 12 minutes or until chicken is tender and no longer pink, turning once and brushing with glaze the last 5 minutes of broiling. (Or, grill chicken on the rack of an uncovered grill directly over medium coals for 12 to 15 minutes or until chicken is tender and no longer pink, turning once halfway through grilling time and brushing with glaze the last 5 minutes of grilling.)

Meanwhile, lightly coat a large saucepan or Dutch oven with nonstick cooking spray. Heat over medium heat until hot. Add leek, apples, and garlic; cook for 3 minutes. Add the reserved ¼ cup glaze and apple cider or broth; bring to boiling. Add spinach; toss just until wilted. Season to taste with salt and pepper.

To serve, slice the chicken crosswise into 6 to 8 pieces. Divide spinach mixture among 4 serving plates. Top with sliced chicken. Makes 4 servings.

½ cup apple jelly

2 tablespoons soy sauce

1 tablespoon snipped fresh thyme

1 teaspoon finely shredded lemon peel

1 teaspoon grated ginger

4 medium skinless, boneless chicken breast halves

Nonstick cooking spray

⅓ cup sliced leek

2 medium apples, peeled, cored, and chopped

2 cloves garlic, minced

2 tablespoons apple cider or chicken broth

1 10-ounce package prewashed fresh spinach, trimmed (about 8 cups)

Nutrition Facts per serving: 263 cal., 3 g total fat (1 g sat. fat), 45 mg chol., 654 mg sodium, 42 g carbo., 4 g fiber, 19 g pro. ▶ Exchanges: 3 Vegetable, 1 Fruit, 2 Meat

Nutrition Facts per serving: 175 cal., 3 g total fat (1 g sat. fat), 60 mg chol., 551 mg sodium, 10 g carbo., 0 g fiber, 22 g pro. ▶ Exchanges: 3 Meat

4 medium skinless, boneless chicken breast halves (about 1 pound total)

4 green onions, thinly sliced (½ cup)

½ cup rice wine or dry sherry

⅓ cup oyster sauce

2 teaspoons finely shredded lime peel

¼ cup lime juice

2 tablespoons chili paste

4 cloves garlic, minced

2 tablespoons honey

Hot cooked rice (optional)

Place chicken in a plastic bag set in a shallow dish. For marinade, stir together green onions, rice wine or sherry, oyster sauce, lime peel, lime juice, chili paste, and garlic. Pour over chicken; seal bag. Marinate in the refrigerator for 6 to 8 hours, turning bag occasionally.

Drain chicken, reserving 1 cup of the marinade; discard remaining marinade. Pour reserved marinade into a small saucepan. Bring to boiling. Cook, uncovered, about 5 minutes or until reduced to ½ cup. Remove from heat; stir in honey.

Grill chicken on the rack of an uncovered grill directly over medium coals for 12 to 15 minutes or until chicken is tender and no longer pink, turning once halfway through grilling time, and brushing with hot marinade the last 5 minutes of grilling.

To serve, cut the chicken breasts diagonally into slices. If desired, serve with hot cooked rice. Makes 4 servings.

Lime juice tenderizes this grilled chicken and brings the flavor of your favorite Thai restaurant to your table.

thai grilled chicken

Although most of the alcohol evaporates during cooking, brandy infuses this dish with a heady, smoky flavor.

4 medium skinless, boneless chicken breast halves (about 1 pound total)

¼ cup all-purpose flour

¼ teaspoon salt

⅛ teaspoon ground red pepper

1 tablespoon olive oil

1 tablespoon margarine or butter

3 medium nectarines or plums, pitted and cut into thin wedges

3 tablespoons brandy

2 tablespoons water

1 tablespoon lemon juice

2 tablespoons sliced almonds, toasted

Place each chicken breast half between 2 pieces of plastic wrap. Pound lightly with the flat side of a meat mallet, working from the center to the edges until an even ¼-inch thickness is reached. Remove plastic wrap. In a pie plate or shallow dish combine flour, salt, and red pepper. Coat chicken pieces with flour mixture.

In a large skillet heat oil and butter or margarine over medium heat. Add chicken; cook for 6 to 8 minutes or until chicken is tender and no longer pink, turning once. Remove skillet from heat. Transfer chicken to a serving platter; cover and keep warm. Add the nectarines or plums, brandy, water, and lemon juice to the skillet. Return skillet to heat and cook for 1 minute, stirring gently.

To serve, spoon fruit mixture over chicken. Sprinkle with almonds. Makes 4 servings.

ADD FUN TO YOUR LIFE ▶ MIND·BODY·SPIRIT

Choosing pleasurable activities is key to a rich and fulfilling life. People who are happiest are those who have an active social life. Those who do things simply to pass the time don't claim to have as great a sense of well-being. So the next time you're having a bad day, call up a couple of your friends and go for a walk.

Nutrition Facts per serving: 303 cal., 12 g total fat (3 g sat. fat), 67 mg chol., 217 mg sodium, 19 g carbo., 2 g fiber, 24 g pro. ▶ Exchanges: 1 Fruit, 3 Meat, 1½ Fat

Nutrition Facts per serving: 304 cal., 14 g total fat (2 g sat. fat), 59 mg chol., 268 mg sodium, 22 g carbo., 5 g fiber, 24 g pro. ▶ Exchanges: 1 Vegetable, 1 Fruit, 3 Meat, 1 Fat

4 medium skinless, boneless chicken breast halves

1 recipe Citrus-Spice Marinade

1 medium orange, sliced

1 small sweet onion, cut into ½-inch slices

1 small eggplant, cut into 1-inch slices

1 large red sweet pepper, cut into 1-inch strips

1 medium zucchini or summer squash, quartered lengthwise

Salt and black pepper (optional)

Place chicken in a plastic bag set in a shallow dish; add 1 cup Citrus-Spice Marinade and the orange slices. Refrigerate remaining marinade. Seal bag; turn to coat. Marinate in the refrigerator for 6 to 24 hours, turning bag occasionally.

Remove chicken from bag, discard marinade. Place chicken and vegetables on the rack of an uncovered grill directly over medium coals. Grill chicken for 12 to 15 minutes or until tender and no longer pink, turning and brushing with remaining marinade halfway through grilling time. Grill the vegetables for 8 to 10 minutes or until tender, brushing occasionally with marinade. If desired, season vegetables with salt and pepper. Makes 4 servings.

Citrus-Spice Marinade: In a screw-top jar, combine ¾ cup orange juice; ¼ cup lemon juice; 3 tablespoons cooking oil; 2 tablespoons Worcestershire sauce; 2 cloves garlic, minced; ¾ teaspoon ground cumin; ½ teaspoon onion powder; ¼ teaspoon salt; and ¼ teaspoon pepper. Cover and shake well to mix.

Prepare your ingredients for this grilled dish the night before.
The next day, relax by the grill while the chicken cooks.

grilled citrus chicken

Nutrition Facts per serving: 208 cal., 9 g total fat (2 g sat. fat), 69 mg chol., 425 mg sodium, 7 g carbo., 1 g fiber, 24 g pro. ▶ Exchanges: 1 Vegetable, 3 Meat, ½ Fat

1½ to 2 pounds meaty chicken pieces, skinned

¼ teaspoon salt

⅛ teaspoon black pepper

Nonstick cooking spray

1 clove garlic, minced

1 lemon, thinly sliced

1 large tomato, peeled and chopped (¾ cup)

½ cup pitted ripe olives

¼ cup chopped onion

¼ cup snipped fresh parsley

1 tablespoon snipped fresh oregano or 1 teaspoon dried oregano, crushed

⅛ teaspoon ground red pepper

¼ cup dry white wine or chicken broth

¾ cup chicken broth

1 medium green sweet pepper, cut into strips

1 medium red sweet pepper, cut into strips

Sprinkle chicken with salt and pepper. Lightly coat a nonstick skillet with nonstick cooking spray. Cook chicken over medium heat about 15 minutes or until light brown, turning once. Reduce heat.

Place the garlic, half of the lemon slices, half of the tomato, the olives, onion, parsley, and oregano over chicken pieces in skillet. Sprinkle with ground red pepper. Add the wine and the ¾ cup broth. Simmer, covered, for 15 minutes.

Add the remaining tomato and the sweet peppers. Cook, covered, for 5 to 10 minutes more or until sweet peppers are crisp-tender and chicken is tender and no longer pink. Transfer the chicken and vegetables to a platter. If desired, garnish with remaining lemon slices. Makes 4 servings.

This meal-in-a-skillet is redolent with the scents of oregano and garlic. Accompany the chicken-and-vegetable mixture with steamed rice.

oregano chicken and vegetables

Nutrition Facts per serving: **241 cal., 4 g total fat (1 g sat. fat), 60 mg chol., 98 mg sodium, 26 g carbo., 1 g fiber, 24 g pro.** ▶ **Exchanges:** 1 Starch, ½ Fruit, 3 Meat

1 **lime**

2 **tangerines**

Nonstick cooking spray

6 **medium** skinless, boneless chicken breast halves

Black pepper

⅓ **cup** chicken broth

¼ **cup** sliced green onions

1 **teaspoon** snipped fresh rosemary or basil or ¼ teaspoon dried rosemary or basil, crushed

1 **tablespoon** water

½ **teaspoon** cornstarch

3 **cups** hot cooked rice or couscous

Finely shred lime peel; measure ½ teaspoon peel. Set peel aside. Finely shred tangerine peel; measure 1 teaspoon peel. Set peel aside. Halve lime and squeeze 1 tablespoon juice; set juice aside. Peel and section tangerines over a bowl to catch juices; set aside.

Lightly coat a large skillet with nonstick cooking spray. Season chicken with pepper. Cook chicken in skillet over medium heat for 5 minutes or until browned, turning once. Add broth, green onions, rosemary or basil, reserved peels, and lime juice. Bring to boiling; reduce heat. Simmer, covered, about 8 minutes or until chicken is tender and no longer pink. Remove chicken from skillet; keep warm.

For sauce, combine water and cornstarch; add to juices in skillet. Cook and stir until thickened and bubbly. Cook and stir for 2 minutes more. Add tangerine sections and any juice; heat through. Pour sauce over chicken. Serve with hot cooked rice or couscous. Makes 6 servings.

lime and tangerine chicken

Tangerine and lime pair up for a lively yet simple chicken dish. Serve with couscous or rice and steamed carrots for a midweek meal.

creamy chicken enchiladas

You won't believe a dish this low in fat is so rich in flavor until you taste your first luscious bite.

Place chicken in a large saucepan in enough water to cover. Bring to boiling; reduce heat. Simmer, covered, about 15 minutes or until chicken is tender and no longer pink. Remove chicken from saucepan. When cool enough to handle, use a fork to shred chicken into bite-size pieces (you should have about 1½ cups). Set aside.

In a saucepan cook fresh spinach, covered, in a small amount of boiling water for 3 to 5 minutes. (If using frozen spinach, do not cook it.) Drain spinach well.

In a large bowl combine chicken, spinach, and green onions; set aside. For sauce, in a bowl combine sour cream, yogurt, flour, cumin, and salt. Stir in milk and chile peppers. Set aside.

For filling, combine half of the sauce and the chicken-spinach mixture. Divide filling among tortillas; roll up. Place filled tortillas, seam sides down, in an ungreased 2-quart rectangular baking dish.

Spoon remaining sauce over tortillas. Bake, uncovered, in a 350° oven about 25 minutes or until heated through. Sprinkle with cheese; let stand for 5 minutes. If desired, garnish with chopped tomato or salsa and additional green onions. Makes 6 servings.

8 ounces skinless, boneless chicken breast halves

4 cups torn fresh spinach or ½ of one 10-ounce package frozen chopped spinach, thawed and drained

2 green onions, thinly sliced (¼ cup)

1 8-ounce carton light dairy sour cream

¼ cup plain fat-free yogurt

2 tablespoons all-purpose flour

¼ teaspoon ground cumin

¼ teaspoon salt

½ cup fat-free milk

1 4½-ounce can diced green chile peppers, drained

6 7-inch flour tortillas

⅓ cup shredded reduced-fat cheddar cheese

Chopped tomato or salsa (optional)

Nutrition Facts per serving: 248 cal., 7 g total fat (2 g sat. fat), 28 mg chol., 412 mg sodium, 29 g carbo., 1 g fiber, 17 g pro. ▶ Exchanges: 1½ Starch, 1 Vegetable, 1½ Meat, ½ Fat

1 tablespoon olive oil

1 teaspoon lemon juice

¼ teaspoon paprika

Dash salt

Dash freshly ground black pepper

4 medium skinless, boneless chicken breast halves

2 whole wheat pita bread rounds, split and toasted

1 recipe Hummus

¾ cup coarsely chopped tomato

½ cup chopped cucumber

Fresh cilantro (optional)

Plain fat-free yogurt (optional)

In a small bowl combine the oil, lemon juice, paprika, salt, and pepper; set aside.

Place chicken on the unheated rack of a broiler pan. Brush both sides of chicken with the oil mixture. Broil 4 to 5 inches from heat for 10 to 12 minutes or until chicken is tender and no longer pink, turning once. Cool chicken slightly; coarsely chop chicken.

To serve, spread Hummus over the toasted pita halves. Top with the chicken, tomatoes, and cucumber. If desired, garnish with cilantro and serve with yogurt. Makes 4 servings.

Hummus: In a blender container or food processor bowl combine one 15-ounce can garbanzo beans, drained and rinsed; ½ cup chopped fresh cilantro; 3 tablespoons lemon juice or lime juice; 3 tablespoons water; 2 cloves garlic, peeled and halved; ⅛ teaspoon salt; and a dash bottled hot pepper sauce. Cover and blend or process until smooth. Refrigerate until ready to serve. Makes about 1⅓ cups.

Make the hummus and chicken the day before. The next day, have a great lunch ready to go.

mediterranean
tostadas

Nutrition Facts per serving: 175 cal., 4 g total fat (1 g sat. fat), 93 mg chol., 119 mg sodium, 2 g carbo., 0 g fiber, 32 g pro. ▶ Exchanges: 4 Meat

3 cups hickory or mesquite wood chips (optional)

Nonstick cooking spray

2 tablespoons chopped onion

2 tablespoons brown mustard

2 teaspoons brown sugar

½ teaspoon chili powder

⅛ teaspoon ground cumin

⅛ teaspoon black pepper

1 2- to 2¼-pound turkey breast half with bone

If desired, at least 1 hour before cooking, soak wood chips in enough water to cover.

Lightly coat a small skillet with nonstick cooking spray. Cook onion over medium heat until tender. Stir in the brown mustard, brown sugar, chili powder, cumin, and pepper; cook for 1 minute more. With your fingers, make a pocket under the skin of the turkey breast. Spread onion mixture evenly under the skin. Insert a meat thermometer into turkey breast.

Drain wood chips, if using. Arrange medium-hot coals around a drip pan. Sprinkle about 1 cup of the wood chips over coals. Place turkey on a grill rack in a roasting pan. Cover and grill about 1¼ hours or until the thermometer registers 170°. Add more coals and wood chips every 20 to 30 minutes. Remove turkey from grill. Cover with foil and let stand for 15 minutes before carving. Makes 6 servings.

Flavor goes right to the meat when you slip a mustard-chili-onion mixture under the turkey skin. Grilling adds another flavor dimension.

chili-mustard turkey

pasta with arugula and sausage

Not a meek or mild green, arugula is somewhat bitter with a peppery mustard flavor. Substitute spinach for those with delicate taste buds.

Cut sausage lengthwise into quarters; cut into ¼-inch pieces. In a large skillet cook leek and garlic in hot olive oil until tender. Stir in sausage pieces, chicken broth, and roasted sweet peppers. Bring to boiling; reduce heat. Add arugula or spinach and cook for 1 to 2 minutes or until greens are wilted. Remove from heat.

Meanwhile, cook pasta according to package directions; drain. Toss pasta with sausage mixture, basil, Parmesan cheese, and pepper. Makes 4 servings.

4 ounces cooked smoked turkey sausage or chicken sausage

1 large leek, cut into ¼-inch slices

2 cloves garlic, minced

1 teaspoon olive oil

⅔ cup reduced-sodium chicken broth

½ of a 7-ounce jar roasted red sweet peppers, drained and cut into bite-size strips

8 cups torn fresh arugula or spinach

6 ounces dried medium bow ties

¼ cup snipped fresh basil

¼ cup finely shredded Parmesan cheese

½ teaspoon coarsely cracked black pepper

MIND·BODY·SPIRIT ▶ TUNING OUT PAIN

Music has been shown to ease tension, and now it seems melodies may ease a patient's postoperative pain. In hospital experiments, the combination of music and pain medication worked better than medicine alone. Do you have a horrific headache? Try listening to a relaxing CD instead of popping a pain pill.

Nutrition Facts per serving: 267 cal., 6 g total fat (2 g sat. fat), 24 mg chol., 473 mg sodium, 38 g carbo., 2 g fiber, 15 g pro. ▶ Exchanges: 2 Starch, 1½ Vegetable, 1 Meat, ½ Fat

Fettuccine, ginger, and sugar snap peas come together for a satisfying meal that delivers on taste and nutrition.

In a small bowl combine dried mushrooms and 1 cup warm water; let stand for 15 minutes. Drain mushrooms, squeezing out excess liquid; reserve liquid. Slice mushroom caps; discard stems. Stir cornstarch into reserved mushroom liquid.

Meanwhile, cook pasta according to package directions. Drain; keep warm.

In a bowl stir together the chicken, sherry, soy sauce, ginger, and garlic; set aside.

Lightly coat a wok or large skillet with nonstick cooking spray. Heat wok or skillet over medium-high heat. Stir-fry sugar snap peas and carrots for 3 to 4 minutes or until crisp-tender. Add green onions and stir-fry for 1 minute more. Remove vegetables from wok; set aside. Add chicken mixture to wok. Stir-fry for 2 to 4 minutes or until chicken is no longer pink. Push chicken from center of wok. Stir cornstarch mixture; add to center of wok. Cook and stir until thickened and bubbly.

Return vegetables to wok. Add mushrooms and pasta. Stir to coat with sauce. Cook and stir for 1 minute or until heated through. If desired, garnish with green onion curls. Makes 4 servings.

1 ounce **dried shiitake mushrooms**

1 tablespoon **cornstarch**

6 ounces **dried fettuccine**

12 ounces **skinless, boneless chicken breast halves, cut into bite-size pieces**

2 tablespoons **dry sherry**

2 tablespoons **light soy sauce**

1 tablespoon **grated fresh ginger**

2 cloves **garlic, minced**

Nonstick cooking spray

1 cup **sugar snap peas (strings and tips removed)**

8 ounces **tiny whole carrots with tops (about 12), trimmed**

4 **green onions, bias-sliced into 1-inch pieces**

Green onion strips (optional)

Nutrition Facts per serving: 333 cal., 3 g total fat (1 g sat. fat), 45 mg chol., 324 mg sodium, 48 g carbo., 3 g fiber, 25 g pro. ▶ Exchanges: 2½ Starch, 1 Vegetable, 2 Meat

Turn your charcoal grill into a smoker and infuse the lean turkey breast with mesquite flavor. Rhubarb chutney is the crowning glory.

smoked turkey with rhubarb chutney

4 cups **mesquite wood chips**

1 3- to 3½-pound **turkey breast half with bone**

⅓ cup **chopped onion**

1 clove **garlic, minced**

¼ cup **dried cherries or golden raisins**

¼ cup **packed brown sugar**

1¼ cups **water**

2 tablespoons **cider vinegar**

1 teaspoon **grated fresh ginger**

⅛ teaspoon **salt**

Dash **ground red pepper**

1½ cups **½-inch pieces rhubarb**

At least 1 hour before grilling, soak wood chips in enough water to cover. Drain chips. Arrange preheated coals around a drip pan in a covered grill. Pour 1 inch of water into pan. Sprinkle half of drained chips onto preheated coals. Test for medium heat above pan. Insert a meat thermometer into the thickest part of turkey, making sure bulb does not touch bone. Place turkey on grill rack over drip pan. Cover; grill for 45 minutes. Add more drained chips and coals. Cover; grill for ¾ to 1¼ hours more or until thermometer registers 170°, adding coals every 45 minutes. Remove from grill. Cover; let stand 15 minutes before carving.

In a saucepan bring onion, garlic, cherries, brown sugar, water, vinegar, ginger, salt, red pepper to boiling; reduce heat. Simmer, covered, for 10 minutes. Add rhubarb. Simmer, covered, for 5 minutes. Uncover; simmer 5 to 10 minutes more or until of desired consistency. Cool. Serve with turkey. Makes 6 to 8 servings.

Nutrition Facts per serving: 200 cal., 1 g total fat (0 g sat. fat), 79 mg chol., 100 mg sodium, 18 g carbo., 1 g fiber, 29 g pro. ▶ Exchanges: ½ Fruit, ½ Starch, 4 Meat

Nutrition Facts per serving: 174 cal., 4 g total fat (1 g sat. fat), 59 mg chol., 466 mg sodium, 11 g carbo., 1 g fiber, 23 g pro. ▶ Exchanges: ½ Fruit, 3 Meat

1   1½-pound fresh or frozen
    salmon fillet (with
    skin), 1 inch thick

2   tablespoons sugar

2½ teaspoons finely
    shredded orange peel

1   teaspoon salt

¼   teaspoon freshly ground
    black pepper

2   oranges, peeled,
    sectioned, and coarsely
    chopped

1   cup chopped fresh
    pineapple or canned
    crushed pineapple,
    drained

2   tablespoons snipped fresh
    cilantro

1   tablespoon finely
    chopped shallot

1   fresh jalapeño pepper,
    seeded and finely
    chopped (2 teaspoons)

Thaw fish, if frozen. Rinse fish; pat dry. Place fish skin side down in a shallow dish. For rub, in a small bowl stir together sugar, 1½ teaspoons of the orange peel, the salt, and pepper. Sprinkle mixture evenly over fish (not on skin side); rub in with your fingers. Cover and refrigerate for 8 to 24 hours.

Meanwhile, for salsa, in a small bowl combine the remaining 1 teaspoon orange peel, oranges, pineapple, cilantro, shallot, and jalapeño pepper. Cover and chill until ready to serve or up to 24 hours.

Arrange medium-hot coals around a drip pan. Test for medium heat above the drip pan. Drain fish, discarding liquid. Place fish skin side down on greased grill rack over drip pan. Cover and grill about 12 minutes or until fish flakes easily when tested with a fork.

To serve, cut fish into 6 serving-size pieces, cutting to, but not through, the skin. Carefully slip a metal spatula between fish and skin, lifting fish up and away from skin. Serve fish with salsa. Makes 6 servings.

A sugar-and-orange-peel rub caramelizes while the salmon grills, giving the salmon a beautiful golden-brown coating.

caramelized salmon
with citrus salsa

salmon with wilted greens

A splash of toasted sesame oil adds a delicious, nutty nuance to the orange dressing.

Thaw fish, if frozen. Rinse fish; pat dry. For dressing, in a small bowl combine orange juice concentrate, soy sauce, honey, cooking oil, sesame oil, ginger, and 3 tablespoons water.

Place fish on the greased unheated rack of a broiler pan. Broil 4 inches from heat for 5 minutes. Using a wide spatula, carefully turn fish over. Brush with 1 tablespoon of the dressing. Broil for 3 to 7 minutes more or until fish flakes easily with a fork. (Or, grill fish on the greased rack of an uncovered grill directly over medium coals for 8 to 12 minutes or until fish flakes easily with a fork, gently turning and brushing once with dressing halfway through grilling time.) Cover and keep fish warm while preparing the greens.

Place greens and orange sections in a large salad bowl. Bring remaining dressing to boiling in a large skillet. Add red pepper strips. Remove from heat. Pour over greens. Toss to mix. Divide among 4 dinner plates. Top each serving with a salmon steak. Serve immediately. Makes 4 servings.

4 6-ounce fresh or frozen salmon steaks, cut 1 inch thick

3 tablespoons orange juice concentrate

2 tablespoons light soy sauce

1 tablespoon honey

2 teaspoons cooking oil

1 teaspoon toasted sesame oil

½ teaspoon grated fresh ginger or ¼ teaspoon ground ginger

6 cups torn mixed greens (such as spinach, Swiss chard, mustard, beet, or collard greens)

1 medium orange, peeled and sectioned

1 small red sweet pepper, cut into thin strips

Nutrition Facts per serving: 256 cal., 9 g total fat (2 g sat. fat), 31 mg chol., 429 mg sodium, 15 g carbo., 2 g fiber, 27 g pro. ▶ Exchanges: 2 Vegetable, ½ Fruit, 3 Meat

fish tacos with mango salsa

Strips of swordfish mingle with jerk seasoning and mango salsa for a different kind of taco.

Thaw fish, if frozen. Rinse fish; pat dry. Cut fish crosswise into ¾-inch slices; sprinkle with Jamaican jerk seasoning. Place fish strips in a greased grill basket. Grill fish on the rack of an uncovered grill directly over medium-hot coals for 8 to 10 minutes or until fish flakes easily with a fork, turning the basket once halfway through grilling time.

Meanwhile, wrap tortillas in foil. Place at edge of grill; heat for 10 minutes, turning occasionally.

To serve, fill warm tortillas with spinach, fish, and Mango Salsa. Makes 8 servings.

Mango Salsa: In a large bowl combine 1 large mango, peeled, seeded, and chopped; 1 large tomato, seeded and chopped; 1 small cucumber, seeded and chopped; 2 tablespoons snipped fresh cilantro; 1 jalapeño pepper, seeded and chopped; 1 thinly sliced green onion; and 1 tablespoon lime juice. Cover; refrigerate until serving time. Serve with a slotted spoon. Makes about 3 cups.

Broiling directions: Place seasoned fish slices on the greased unheated rack of a broiler pan. Broil 4 inches from the heat for 5 minutes; turn fish. Broil for 3 to 7 minutes more or until fish flakes easily with a fork. Meanwhile, wrap tortillas in foil. Heat package on lower rack of oven for 5 to 7 minutes.

1 pound **fresh or frozen swordfish or halibut steaks, cut 1 inch thick**

½ teaspoon **Jamaican jerk seasoning**

8 6-inch **flour tortillas**

2 cups **shredded fresh spinach or lettuce**

1 recipe **Mango Salsa**

Fresh spinach leaves (optional)

Nutrition Facts per serving: 418 cal., 10 g total fat (2 g sat. fat), 45 mg chol., 463 mg sodium, 52 g carbo., 3 g fiber, 30 g pro. ▶ Exchanges: 2 Starch, 1 Vegetable, 1 Fruit, 3 Meat

1½ pounds fresh or frozen fish steaks or fillets (such as sea bass, swordfish, tuna, or salmon), cut 1 inch thick

6 cloves garlic, peeled and quartered

½ of a medium onion, quartered

½ red sweet pepper, cored and seeded

¼ cup dry white wine

2 tablespoons olive oil

2 tablespoons catsup

2 teaspoons sweet paprika

1 teaspoon salt

½ teaspoon freshly ground black pepper

¼ cup snipped fresh cilantro

Thaw fish, if frozen. Rinse fish; pat dry. Place fish in a shallow dish. Set aside. For marinade, in a blender container or food processor bowl combine the garlic, onion, sweet pepper, wine, oil, catsup, paprika, salt, and pepper. Cover and blend or process until smooth; stir in the cilantro.

Pour marinade over fish; turn fish to coat. Cover and marinate in the refrigerator for 2 to 4 hours, turning fish occasionally.

Drain fish, reserving marinade. Grill fish on the greased rack of an uncovered grill directly over medium coals for 8 to 12 minutes or until fish flakes easily with a fork, gently turning and brushing once with reserved marinade halfway through grilling time. Makes 4 to 6 servings.

grilled fish with garlic marinade

You'll find dozens of uses for this aromatic marinade, which is easy to make in a blender. Pair it with fish, poultry, or meat.

4 6-ounce fresh or frozen sea bass or halibut fillets, ¾ to 1 inch thick

4 cloves garlic, minced

1 tablespoon grated fresh ginger

¾ teaspoon salt

½ teaspoon ground cardamom

2 teaspoons toasted sesame oil

4 teaspoons lemon juice

1 medium red onion, sliced ¼ inch thick

1 tablespoon olive oil

2 jalapeño peppers, seeded and finely chopped

3 small yellow or red tomatoes, halved and cut into wedges

1 tablespoon snipped fresh oregano

¾ teaspoon snipped fresh thyme

¼ teaspoon black pepper

Thaw fish, if frozen. Rinse fish; pat dry. Set aside.

For paste, stir together half of the garlic, the ginger, ½ teaspoon of the salt, the cardamom, and sesame oil. With your fingers, rub both sides of fish evenly with paste. Let fish stand at room temperature for 15 minutes. Just before grilling, drizzle lemon juice over fish. Grill fish on the greased rack of an uncovered grill directly over medium coals for 6 to 9 minutes or until fish flakes easily with a fork, turning once halfway through grilling time.

Meanwhile, in a large, heavy skillet cook onion slices in hot olive oil over medium-high heat until tender, stirring frequently. Add remaining garlic and the jalapeño peppers; continue cooking until onions are golden. Add tomatoes, oregano, thyme, pepper, and remaining ¼ teaspoon salt. Stir gently until heated through.

To serve, place fish on a serving platter; top with the tomato-onion mixture. Makes 4 servings.

Rub the fish with a garlic and ginger sesame oil mixture before grilling and smother it with a tomato-onion-hot pepper medley.

grilled chorrillos-style sea bass

coconut-curry shrimp

Using cut-up vegetables from the salad bar or packaged stir-fry vegetables saves you the time it takes to clean and chop fresh vegetables.

12 ounces fresh or frozen medium shrimp in shells

1 14½-ounce can reduced-sodium chicken broth

¾ cup water

1 cup quick-cooking couscous

2 teaspoons cooking oil

3 cups assorted fresh vegetables, such as broccoli flowerets; sweet pepper, carrot, or zucchini strips; and/or sliced fresh mushrooms

1 small onion or 2 large shallots, chopped

3 cloves garlic, minced

1 tablespoon all-purpose flour

2 to 3 teaspoons curry powder

¼ teaspoon salt

⅛ to ¼ teaspoon ground red pepper

½ cup light coconut milk

Condiments, such as chopped peanuts, golden raisins, mango chutney, and/or snipped cilantro (optional)

Thaw shrimp, if frozen. Peel and devein shrimp; set aside.

Set aside 1 cup of the chicken broth. In a medium saucepan bring remaining broth and the water to boiling. Stir in couscous. Cover and remove from heat. Let stand while preparing curry.

In a large, deep nonstick skillet heat oil over medium-high heat. Add desired vegetables, onion or shallots, and garlic; stir-fry for 2 minutes. Stir in the flour, curry powder, salt, and red pepper. Cook for 1 minute, stirring constantly. Carefully stir in the reserved 1 cup broth and the coconut milk. Cook and stir until thickened and bubbly. Stir in shrimp. Return just to boiling; reduce heat. Simmer, covered, about 3 minutes or until shrimp are opaque and vegetables are tender.

To serve, ladle into 4 shallow bowls; top each serving with couscous. If desired, serve with peanuts, raisins, chutney, or cilantro. Makes 4 servings.

Nutrition Facts per serving: 320 cal., 6 g total fat (2 g sat. fat), 131 mg chol., 593 mg sodium, 44 g carbo., 9 g fiber, 23 g pro. ▶ Exchanges: 2½ Starch, 1 Vegetable, 2 Meat

Nutrition Facts per serving: 101 cal., 2 g total fat (0 g sat. fat), 103 mg chol., 320 mg sodium, 3 g carbo., 1 g fiber, 17 g pro. ▶ Exchanges: ½ Vegetable, 2 Meat

8 ounces fresh or frozen large shrimp in shells

8 ounces fresh or frozen sea scallops or 10 ounces fresh or frozen halibut steaks

Parchment paper or aluminum foil

2 medium plum tomatoes, seeded and chopped

1 tablespoon dry vermouth or dry white wine (optional)

1½ teaspoons snipped fresh basil or ½ teaspoon dried basil, crushed

1½ teaspoons snipped fresh thyme or ½ teaspoon dried thyme, crushed

1 teaspoon olive oil

¼ teaspoon salt

Pinch thread saffron, crushed, or ¼ teaspoon ground turmeric

1 clove garlic, minced

1 small zucchini, halved lengthwise and thinly sliced

4 green onions, cut into 1-inch pieces

Hot cooked rice or couscous (optional)

Thaw shrimp and scallops or halibut, if frozen. Peel and devein shrimp. Halve any large scallops or skin, bone, and cut halibut into 1-inch pieces. Set aside.

Cut four 12-inch squares from parchment paper or aluminum foil. Fold each square in half to form a triangle. Open each triangle to lie flat.

In a large bowl combine tomatoes, vermouth or wine (if desired), basil, thyme, olive oil, salt, saffron or turmeric, and garlic. Add shrimp, scallops or halibut, zucchini, and green onions; toss to coat. Spoon mixture onto the center of one side of each triangle. Fold the paper over the mixture. Fold each of the open sides over ½ inch, then fold over again ½ inch.

Place packages on a baking sheet. Bake in a 400° oven for 10 to 12 minutes or until shrimp and scallops are opaque or halibut flakes easily when tested with a fork. If desired, serve with rice or couscous. Makes 4 servings.

Cooking in a parchment packet allows the scallops, shrimp, and vegetables to stay moist and tender, and makes cleanup a snap.

cioppino seafood en papillote

Grow fresh basil year-round in a sunny window. Its distinctive flavor adds character to sauces like this one.

6 ounces dried campanelle or other pasta (such as bow tie or mostaccioli)

1 cup shelled fresh peas or frozen peas, thawed

1 12-ounce can (1½ cups) evaporated fat-free milk

1 tablespoon all-purpose flour

2 tablespoons snipped fresh basil

1 clove garlic, minced

¼ cup shredded Parmesan cheese

2 ounces prosciutto, chopped

2 tablespoons shredded Parmesan cheese

Black pepper (optional)

Fresh basil leaves (optional)

Cook pasta according to package directions; drain.

Meanwhile, in a medium saucepan cook shelled peas, if using, in a small amount of boiling water for 10 minutes. Drain; return to saucepan. Stir together the evaporated milk and flour; add to cooked peas in saucepan. Stir in basil and garlic.

Cook and stir over medium heat until mixture is thickened and bubbly. Cook and stir for 1 minute more. Add the ¼ cup Parmesan cheese, the prosciutto, and, if using, the thawed peas; stir until cheese is melted. Do not boil. Pour over cooked pasta; gently toss to coat. Top with the 2 tablespoons Parmesan cheese and pepper. If desired, garnish with basil. Makes 4 servings.

Note: If using frozen peas, add to evaporated milk mixture after it has been thickened.

Nutrition Facts per serving: 337 cal., 8 g total fat (0 g sat. fat), 47 mg chol., 478 mg sodium, 45 g carbo., 1 g fiber, 21 g pro. ▶ Exchanges: 2½ Starch, 1 Meat, ½ Milk, 1 Fat

Nutrition Facts per serving: 191 cal., 12 g total fat (3 g sat. fat), 51 mg chol., 343 mg sodium, 2 g carbo., 1 g fiber, 18 g pro. ▶ Exchanges: 2½ Meat, ½ Fat

4 boneless pork loin chops, cut 1 inch thick (about 1 pound total)

½ cup spicy brown mustard

¼ cup dry white wine

1 tablespoon curry powder

1 tablespoon olive oil

¼ to ½ teaspoon crushed red pepper

1 green onion, sliced

1 clove garlic, minced

Trim fat from pork chops. Place chops in a plastic bag set in a shallow dish. For marinade, stir together the mustard, wine, curry powder, oil, red pepper, green onion, and garlic. Pour marinade over chops in bag; seal bag. Marinate in the refrigerator for 6 to 24 hours, turning the bag occasionally.

Drain chops, reserving the marinade. Arrange preheated coals around a drip pan. Test for medium heat above pan. Place chops on the grill rack over drip pan. Cover and grill chops for 30 to 35 minutes or until a meat thermometer inserted in the center of each chop registers 160°, turning and brushing once with marinade halfway through grilling. Discard any remaining marinade. Makes 4 servings.

To keep lean pork chops succulent, marinate and glaze the meat with a sweet and spicy mustard mixture.

curry-mustard pork chops

mojo pork roast

For an easy menu when entertaining, add steamed green beans and rice to this Cuban-inspired roast.

Trim fat from pork roast. Place meat in a plastic bag in a shallow dish. For marinade, in a small bowl combine orange juice, lime juice, sugar, oregano, and garlic. Pour the marinade over the meat; seal bag. Marinate in the refrigerator overnight, turning bag occasionally.

Drain meat, discarding marinade. Place meat on a rack in a shallow roasting pan. Insert a meat thermometer. Sprinkle the meat with salt and pepper. Roast in a 350° oven for 45 to 60 minutes or until the thermometer registers 160°. Cover meat with foil; let stand for 5 minutes before slicing. Makes 4 servings.

MIND·BODY·SPIRIT ▶ JUMP FOR YOUR BONES

Jumping rope three times a week may increase your bone density. And if you have arthritis, your pain may ease as your joint stability improves. For the most benefit, do at least 50 jumps at a comfortable pace, jump no more than 5 inches in the air, and land flat-footed to distribute the force.

1 1-pound boneless pork top loin roast (single loin)

⅓ cup orange juice

¼ cup lime juice

1 teaspoon sugar

1 teaspoon dried oregano, crushed

3 cloves garlic, minced

¼ teaspoon salt

¼ teaspoon black pepper

Nutrition Facts per serving: 147 cal., 7 g total fat (3 g sat. fat), 51 mg chol., 173 mg sodium, 3 g carbo., 0 g fiber, 16 g pro. ▶ Exchanges: 2½ Meat

sweet pepper and olive pork

A family favorite gets a Latino twist. Pimiento-stuffed olives are often sold already chopped for ease. Look for "salad olives" on the label.

Nonstick cooking spray

1 12-ounce pork loin tenderloin, cut into eight ¼-inch slices

⅛ teaspoon salt

⅛ teaspoon black pepper

2 teaspoons olive oil

2 medium onions, cut into thin wedges

2 medium green sweet peppers, cut into thin bite-size strips

½ cup sliced fresh mushrooms

2 cloves garlic, minced

½ teaspoon ground cumin

⅓ cup chopped pimiento-stuffed green olives

Lightly coat a large skillet with nonstick cooking spray; heat over medium-high heat. Season pork slices with salt and pepper. Cook half of the pork slices at a time in skillet for 2 to 3 minutes or until meat is browned and juices run clear, turning once. Remove slices from skillet; keep warm.

Add olive oil to skillet; heat over medium-high heat. Cook onions, sweet peppers, mushrooms, garlic, and cumin in skillet about 4 minutes or until crisp-tender.

Stir in olives; heat through. Serve vegetable mixture with pork slices. Makes 4 servings.

Nutrition Facts per serving: 171 cal., 9 g total fat (2 g sat. fat), 38 mg chol., 342 mg sodium, 9 g carbo., 2 g fiber, 14 g pro. ▶ Exchanges: 1 Vegetable, 1½ Meat, 1 Fat

Nutrition Facts per serving: 255 cal., 7 g total fat (2 g sat. fat), 60 mg chol., 179 mg sodium, 29 g carbo., 3 g fiber, 19 g pro. ▶ Exchanges: 1 Starch, 1 Fruit, 2 Meat

Cut tenderloin crosswise into ¼-inch slices. Combine rosemary, thyme, salt, and pepper; sprinkle over pork slices. In a large skillet cook pork slices, half at a time, in hot oil for 2 to 3 minutes or until meat is browned and juices run clear, turning meat once. Remove meat from skillet; set aside.

In the same skillet combine pears, maple syrup, white wine or apple juice, and cherries. Bring to boiling; reduce heat. Boil gently, uncovered, about 3 minutes or until the pears are just tender. Return pork slices to skillet with pear mixture; heat through.

To serve, transfer pork slices to a warm serving platter; spoon pear mixture over pork. Makes 4 servings.

1 12- to 16-ounce **pork tenderloin**

2 teaspoons **snipped fresh rosemary** or ½ teaspoon **dried rosemary, crushed**

1 teaspoon **snipped fresh thyme** or ¼ teaspoon **dried thyme, crushed**

¼ teaspoon **salt**

¼ teaspoon **black pepper**

1 tablespoon **olive oil** or **cooking oil**

2 medium **pears, peeled, cored, and coarsely chopped**

¼ cup **maple syrup** or **maple-flavored syrup**

2 tablespoons **dry white wine** or **apple juice**

2 tablespoons **dried tart red cherries, halved**

pork with pear-maple sauce

Succulent pears, tart cherries, and maple syrup create a tantalizing sauce for these tender slices of pork.

91

pork spirals with red pepper sauce

These pork spirals will garner requests for seconds from guests. The red pepper sauce is versatile enough for chicken, beef, or fish.

Trim fat from meat. Using a sharp knife, make a lengthwise cut along the center of the tenderloin, cutting to, but not through, the oppostie side. Spread meat open. Place meat between two pieces of plastic wrap. Working from center to the edges, use flat side of a meat mallet to pound meat into an 11×7-inch rectangle. Remove plastic. Fold in narrow ends as necessary to make an even rectangle.

Stack spinach leaves on top of each other; slice crosswise into thin strips. In a medium bowl stir together spinach, mushrooms, basil, bread crumbs, Parmesan cheese, and egg white. Spread evenly over pork. Starting at one of the short sides, roll up. Tie with 100-percent-cotton string at 1½-inch intervals. Brush surface of meat with 1 teaspoon of the olive oil; sprinkle with pepper.

Arrange medium-hot coals around a drip pan. Test for medium heat above pan. Place meat on grill rack over pan. Cover; grill for 25 to 30 minutes or until a meat thermometer inserted in the center registers 155°. Remove from grill. Cover with foil; let stand for 10 minutes.

Meanwhile, for sauce, in a food processor bowl combine roasted peppers, the remaining 2 teaspoons olive oil, wine vinegar, garlic, and salt. Cover; process until smooth. Transfer sauce to a small saucepan; cook over medium heat until heated through. To serve, remove strings from pork. Slice pork; serve with sauce. Makes 4 servings.

1 12-ounce pork tenderloin

1 cup loosely packed fresh spinach leaves, stems removed

⅓ cup finely chopped fresh mushrooms

¼ cup snipped fresh basil

2 tablespoons fine dry bread crumbs

1 tablespoon finely shredded Parmesan cheese

1 slightly beaten egg white

1 tablespoon olive oil

Black pepper

½ of a 7-ounce jar roasted red sweet peppers, drained

1 teaspoon red or white wine vinegar

1 clove garlic

Dash salt

Nutrition Facts per serving: 176 cal., 7 g total fat (2 g sat. fat), 62 mg chol., 146 mg sodium, 6 g carbo., 1 g fiber, 22 g pro. ▶ Exchanges: 1 Vegetable, 3 Meat

Nutrition Facts per serving: 184 cal., 9 g total fat (3 g sat. fat), 64 mg chol., 181 mg sodium, 2 g carbo., 0 g fiber, 22 g pro. ▶ Exchanges: 3 Meat

2 tablespoons Dijon-style mustard

1 tablespoon snipped fresh rosemary or ½ teaspoon dried rosemary, crushed

1 tablespoon snipped fresh thyme or ½ teaspoon dried thyme, crushed

1 tablespoon snipped fresh basil or 1 teaspoon dried basil, crushed

1 2-pound beef tenderloin

¾ cup soft bread crumbs (1 slice)

1 tablespoon margarine or butter, melted

In a small bowl combine Dijon-style mustard and half of the rosemary, half of the thyme, and half of the basil. Place tenderloin on a rack in a shallow roasting pan. Spread mustard-herb mixture over the tenderloin. Insert a meat thermometer into center of meat. Roast, uncovered, in a 425° oven for 30 to 40 minutes or until the thermometer registers 135°.

Meanwhile, combine bread crumbs, melted margarine or butter, and remaining herbs. Remove roast from oven; sprinkle with crumb mixture, pressing lightly into mustard-herb mixture. Roast for 5 to 10 minutes more or until thermometer registers 140°. Cover meat with foil; let stand for 15 minutes. Slice meat to serve. Makes 8 servings.

Melt-in-your-mouth beef tenderloin enhanced with fresh herbs and mustard makes this a perfect entrée for entertaining.

mustard and herb beef tenderloin

94

bistro beef and mushrooms

Give steak French panache with a mushroom sauce consisting of the classic flavors of mustard, wine, and thyme.

Trim fat from steaks. Spread mustard evenly over both sides of steaks. In a large skillet heat 1 tablespoon of the oil over medium heat. Add steaks to skillet; cook to desired doneness, turning once. (Allow 7 to 10 minutes for medium-rare or 10 to 12 minutes for medium.)

Transfer steaks to a serving platter, reserving drippings in skillet. Keep steaks warm.

Add the remaining 1 tablespoon oil to drippings in skillet. Add mushrooms; cook and stir for 4 minutes. Stir in the wine or sherry, Worcestershire sauce, and thyme. Simmer, uncovered, for 3 minutes. Spoon mushroom mixture over steaks. Makes 4 servings.

4 beef tenderloin steaks, cut ¾ inch thick (1 pound)

1 tablespoon Dijon-style mustard or coarse-grain brown mustard

2 tablespoons roasted garlic olive oil or olive oil

2 4-ounce packages sliced fresh cremini, shiitake, or portobello mushrooms or one 8-ounce package sliced fresh button mushrooms (about 3 cups)

⅓ cup dry red wine or sherry

1 tablespoon white wine Worcestershire sauce

2 teaspoons snipped fresh thyme

Nutrition Facts per serving: 263 cal., 14 g total fat (4 g sat. fat), 64 mg chol., 176 mg sodium, 5 g carbo., 1 g fiber, 23 g pro. ▶ Exchanges: 1 Vegetable, 3 Meat, 1 Fat

Nutrition Facts per serving: 221 cal., 6 g total fat (3 g sat. fat), 40 mg chol., 488 mg sodium, 22 g carbo., 3 g fiber, 20 g pro. ▶ Exchanges: 1½ Starch, 2 Meat

½ of a 15-ounce can (¾ cup) black beans, drained and rinsed

⅔ cup corn relish

¼ cup halved and thinly sliced radishes

1 small fresh jalapeño pepper, seeded and finely chopped

2 teaspoons lime juice

¼ teaspoon ground cumin

1 12-ounce beef flank steak

Salt and black pepper

Fresh rosemary (optional)

For relish, in a small bowl combine drained black beans, corn relish, radishes, jalapeño pepper, lime juice, and cumin. Cover; chill at least 30 minutes or up to 4 hours.

Trim fat from steak. Score both sides of steak in a diamond pattern by making shallow diagonal cuts at 1-inch intervals. Sprinkle with salt and pepper. Place steak on the unheated rack of a broiler pan. Broil 3 to 4 inches from heat for 12 to 14 minutes or to desired doneness, turning once. (Or, grill steak on the rack of an uncovered grill directly over medium coals for 12 to 14 minutes, turning once.)

To serve, thinly slice steak diagonally across the grain. Serve with relish. If desired, garnish with rosemary. Makes 4 servings.

Sizzling steak on the grill is irresistible. Top it with vibrant bean and corn relish and you'll have diners dashing to dinner.

flank steak with bean relish

Nutrition Facts per serving: 217 cal., 10 g total fat (3 g sat. fat), 43 mg chol., 567 mg sodium, 10 g carbo., 1 g fiber, 21 g pro. ▶ Exchanges: ½ Starch, ½ Vegetable, 2½ Meat

1 1- to 1¼-pound beef flank steak

⅓ cup light teriyaki sauce

½ teaspoon bottled hot pepper sauce

4 green onions, cut into 1-inch pieces

1 green or red sweet pepper, cut into ¾-inch pieces

3 tablespoons reduced-fat or regular peanut butter

3 tablespoons water

2 tablespoons light teriyaki sauce

Trim fat from steak. Cut steak diagonally across the grain into thin slices. For marinade, in a medium bowl combine the ⅓ cup teriyaki sauce and ¼ teaspoon of the hot pepper sauce. Add steak slices; toss to coat. Cover and refrigerate for 30 minutes.

Drain steak, reserving marinade. On 10- to 12-inch metal skewers, alternately thread steak strips, accordion style, green onion, and sweet pepper. Brush meat and vegetables with remaining marinade; discard any remaining marinade.

For peanut sauce, in a small saucepan combine the remaining ¼ teaspoon hot pepper sauce, the peanut butter, water, and 2 tablespoons teriyaki sauce. Cook and stir over medium heat just until heated through. Keep warm.

Grill kabobs on the rack of an uncovered grill directly over medium coals for 3 to 4 minutes or until steak is slightly pink in center, turning once halfway through grilling. (Or place skewers on an unheated broiler pan; broil 4 to 5 inches from the heat for 4 minutes, turning once halfway through broiling.) To serve, remove steak and vegetables from skewers; serve with warm peanut sauce. Makes 5 servings.

Fire up your grill for this simplified version of an Indonesian favorite. A quick three-ingredient sauce is the secret for great flavor.

beef satay with peanut sauce

spicy sloppy joes

These are definitely not your mother's sloppy joes. We've added fresh vegetables and herbs to the spicy tomato-meat combination.

In a medium skillet cook the ground beef, onion, and garlic over medium heat until meat is brown. Drain off fat. Stir in zucchini, yellow summer squash, mushrooms, and sweet pepper.

Cover and cook over low heat for 5 to 7 minutes or until vegetables are tender. Stir in salsa, basil, parsley, and rosemary. Simmer, uncovered, about 10 minutes or until most of the liquid has evaporated. Serve meat mixture on toasted rolls. Makes 6 to 8 servings.

1 pound lean ground beef

1 medium onion, chopped

2 cloves garlic, minced

1 cup chopped zucchini

1 cup chopped yellow summer squash

1 cup sliced fresh mushrooms

¾ cup chopped green sweet pepper

1 16-ounce jar salsa

1 teaspoon dried basil, crushed

½ teaspoon dried parsley flakes

½ teaspoon dried rosemary, crushed

6 to 8 Kaiser rolls, split and toasted

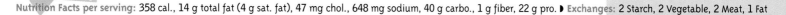

MIND·BODY·SPIRIT ▶ MUSCLE DOWN YOUR WEIGHT

If you haven't added weight training to your workout routine, you might want to give it a try. Women who regularly work out with weights not only increase muscle mass but also boost their metabolism. If you're worried about "bulking up," don't be. Lift lighter weights and do more repetitions to avoid looking like the Hulk.

Nutrition Facts per serving: 358 cal., 14 g total fat (4 g sat. fat), 47 mg chol., 648 mg sodium, 40 g carbo., 1 g fiber, 22 g pro. ▶ Exchanges: 2 Starch, 2 Vegetable, 2 Meat, 1 Fat

baked penne with meat sauce

Stay home and enjoy your favorite Italian dinner.
Freeze this recipe in portion-size containers for almost instant dinners.

Cook pasta according to package directions. Drain well.

Meanwhile, in a blender container or food processor bowl combine undrained tomatoes, tomato paste, wine or tomato juice, sugar, dried oregano (if using), and pepper. Cover and blend or process until smooth. Set aside.

In a large skillet cook ground beef and onion until meat is brown. Drain off fat. Stir in tomato mixture. Bring to boiling; reduce heat. Cover and simmer for 10 minutes. Stir in pasta, fresh oregano (if using), and olives.

Divide the pasta mixture among six 10- to 12-ounce individual casseroles. Bake, covered, in a 375° oven for 15 minutes. (Or, spoon all of the pasta mixture into a 2-quart casserole. Bake, covered, for 30 minutes.) Sprinkle with mozzarella cheese. Bake, uncovered, about 5 minutes more or until cheese is melted. Makes 6 servings.

8 ounces **dried penne**

1 14-ounce can **whole Italian-style tomatoes**

½ of a 6-ounce can (⅓ cup) **Italian-style tomato paste**

¼ cup **dry red wine or tomato juice**

½ teaspoon **sugar**

½ teaspoon **dried oregano, crushed, or 2 teaspoons snipped fresh oregano**

¼ teaspoon **black pepper**

1 pound **lean ground beef**

½ cup **chopped onion**

¼ cup **sliced pitted ripe olives**

½ cup **shredded reduced-fat mozzarella cheese (2 ounces)**

Nutrition Facts per serving: 339 cal., 11 g total fat (4 g sat. fat), 59 mg chol., 349 mg sodium, 33 g carbo., 3 g fiber, 24 g pro. ▶ Exchanges: 1 Vegetable, 2 Starch, 2 Meat, 1 Fat

Nutrition Facts per serving: 257 cal., 9 g total fat (4 g sat. fat), 54 mg chol., 409 mg sodium, 24 g carbo., 3 g fiber, 20 g pro. ◗ Exchanges: 1½ Starch, 2 Meat

½ cup **finely shredded carrot**

¼ cup **thinly sliced green onions**

¼ cup **soft whole wheat bread crumbs**

2 tablespoons **milk**

¼ teaspoon **dried Italian seasoning, crushed**

¼ teaspoon **garlic salt**

Dash **black pepper**

¾ pound **lean ground beef or uncooked ground turkey or chicken**

4 **whole wheat hamburger buns, split and toasted**

Shredded zucchini (optional)

Sliced tomato (optional)

1 recipe **Curry Mustard (optional)**

In a medium bowl stir together carrot, green onions, bread crumbs, milk, Italian seasoning, garlic salt, and pepper. Add the ground beef or turkey or chicken; mix well. Shape meat mixture into four ½-inch-thick patties.

Grill burgers on the rack of an uncovered grill directly over medium coals for 14 to 18 minutes or until an instant-read thermometer inserted into the center of burgers registers 160°, turning once halfway through grilling. (Or, place burgers on unheated rack of a broiler pan. Broil 3 to 4 inches from heat for 12 to 14 minutes or until done, turning once.) To serve, place burgers on buns. If desired, serve burgers with zucchini, tomato, and Curry Mustard. Makes 4 servings.

Curry Mustard: In a small bowl stir together ¼ cup Dijon-style mustard and ½ teaspoon curry powder. Makes ¼ cup.

grilled burgers with curry mustard

Surprise your palate with the flavor of curry and mustard in every bite of these tasty burgers.

tuscan lamb skillet

Forget the mint jelly for these chops. A toss of white beans, tomatoes, olive oil, garlic, and rosemary brings a taste of Italy to your table.

Trim fat from lamb chops. In a large skillet cook chops in hot oil over medium heat about 8 minutes or until a thermometer inserted in center registers 160° for medium doneness, turning once. Transfer chops to a large plate; keep warm.

Stir garlic into drippings in skillet. Cook and stir for 1 minute. Stir in beans, undrained tomatoes, vinegar, and rosemary. Bring to boiling; reduce heat. Simmer, uncovered, for 3 minutes.

Spoon bean mixture onto four dinner plates; arrange two chops on each plate. If desired, garnish with additional rosemary. Makes 4 servings.

8 lamb rib chops, cut 1 inch thick (1½ pounds)

2 teaspoons olive oil

3 cloves garlic, minced

1 19-ounce can white kidney beans, rinsed and drained

1 8-ounce can Italian-style stewed tomatoes

1 tablespoon balsamic vinegar

2 teaspoons snipped fresh rosemary

Fresh rosemary (optional)

Nutrition Facts per serving: 272 cal., 9 g total fat (3 g sat. fat), 67 mg chol., 466 mg sodium, 24 g carbo., 6 g fiber, 30 g pro. ▶ Exchanges: 1½ Starch, 3 Meat

Nutrition Facts per serving: 317 cal., 11 g total fat (4 g sat. fat), 97 mg chol., 83 mg sodium, 24 g carbo., 1 g fiber, 30 g pro. ▶ Exchanges: 1½ Starch, 3½ Meat

8 lamb rib or loin chops, cut 1 inch thick (1½ pounds)

⅓ cup finely chopped shallots

¼ teaspoon crushed red pepper

¼ cup packed brown sugar

¼ cup vinegar

2 tablespoons dried cranberries or currants

½ teaspoon grated fresh ginger

1 medium sweet potato, peeled and cubed

Trim fat from chops. In a small bowl combine shallots and red pepper; reserve 2 tablespoons of the shallot mixture for the chutney. Rub both sides of chops with the remaining shallot mixture. Place chops on the unheated rack of a broiler pan. Set aside.

For chutney, in a medium saucepan combine reserved shallot mixture, the brown sugar, vinegar, cranberries or currants, and ginger. Stir in sweet potato. Bring to boiling; reduce heat. Simmer, covered, for 10 minutes, stirring occasionally.

Meanwhile, broil chops 3 to 4 inches from the heat to desired doneness, turning once. (Allow 7 to 11 minutes for medium doneness or until thermometer registers 160°.) Serve the chops with the chutney. Makes 4 servings.

Serve this dish to company; the rich flavors and beautiful colors of the chutney are guaranteed to wow them.

lamb chops with sweet potato chutney

grilled lamb kabobs

The penetrating flavors of earthy cumin and pungent red pepper make these North-African-inspired lamb kabobs memorable.

Place lamb or beef cubes in a plastic bag set in a deep bowl; set aside. For marinade, in a bowl combine the vinegar, oil, onion, garlic, cumin seed, paprika, thyme, mint, crushed red pepper, salt, and 1 tablespoon water. Pour marinade over meat; seal bag. Marinate in the refrigerator for 6 to 24 hours, turning bag occasionally.

Cook onion wedges, uncovered, in a small amount of boiling water for 3 to 5 minutes or until nearly tender; drain and set aside.

Drain meat, reserving marinade. On eight 6- to 8-inch metal skewers, alternately thread lamb or beef cubes, onion, and red sweet pepper pieces, leaving about ¼ inch between pieces.

Grill kabobs on the rack of an uncovered grill directly over medium coals for 12 to 14 minutes or until desired doneness, turning and brushing once with marinade halfway through grilling. Add cherry tomatoes to skewers; grill for 2 to 3 minutes more. Serve with hot couscous. Makes 4 servings.

1 pound **boneless leg of lamb or boneless beef sirloin steak, cut into 1-inch cubes**

3 tablespoons **vinegar**

1 tablespoon **olive oil**

½ cup **finely chopped onion**

4 cloves **garlic, minced**

2 teaspoons **cumin seed, crushed**

1 teaspoon **paprika**

¾ teaspoon **snipped fresh thyme or ½ teaspoon dried thyme, crushed**

¾ teaspoon **snipped fresh mint or ½ teaspoon dried mint, crushed**

½ teaspoon **crushed red pepper**

¼ teaspoon **salt**

1 medium **red onion, cut into 8 wedges**

1 medium **red sweet pepper, cut into 1-inch pieces**

8 **cherry tomatoes**

2 cups **hot cooked couscous**

Nutrition Facts per serving: 276 cal., 8 g total fat (6 g sat. fat), 63 mg chol., 191 mg sodium, 30 g carbo., 5 g fiber, 21 g pro. ▶ Exchanges: 1½ Starch, 1½ Vegetable, 2 Meat, 1 Fat

CHAPTER FOUR

skip them

eat

peppery artichoke pitas

Hungry and running on empty? Five minutes is all it takes to make these bean-filled sandwiches.

In a medium bowl combine drained beans, artichoke hearts, arugula or spinach, salad dressing, and pepper.

To serve, spoon bean mixture into pita bread halves. Makes 6 servings.

Arugula Tips: Arugula is a peppery, pungent salad green with slender, deep green leaves. It will add a distinctive bite to salads or sandwiches. Wash it gently by immersing it in cold water several times to remove all traces of grit and sand. Pat dry with paper towels. Place the clean arugula in a plastic bag and refrigerate for up to 2 days.

1 15-ounce can Great Northern beans, drained and rinsed

1 13¾- or 14-ounce can artichoke hearts, drained and coarsely chopped

½ cup torn arugula or spinach

¼ cup bottled creamy garlic salad dressing

¼ teaspoon cracked black pepper

3 pita bread rounds, halved crosswise

GOOD CRITICISM ▶ MIND·BODY·SPIRIT

To avoid criticism, do nothing, say nothing, be nothing.—Elbert Hubbard

When we're criticized, it can be devastating, even demoralizing. But it doesn't have to be. First, consider the source; ignore petty jealousy. Otherwise, if it's something you can learn from, listen, take appropriate action, and let it go. Immobilization from criticism will keep you from growing. Taking chances or risks may get you criticized but, in the end, you often will benefit from it.

Nutrition Facts per serving: 227 cal., 5 g total fat (1 g sat. fat), 3 mg chol., 269 mg sodium, 38 g carbo., 6 g fiber, 10 g pro. ▶ **Exchanges:** 2 Starch, 1½ Vegetable, ½ Fat

4   4- to 6-ounce fresh portobello mushrooms

2   tablespoons balsamic vinegar

1   tablespoon extra-virgin olive oil

⅛   teaspoon salt

⅛   teaspoon coarsely ground black pepper

2   red and/or yellow sweet peppers, quartered lengthwise

1   cup chopped tomatoes

½   cup sliced cucumber

½   cup crumbled feta or goat cheese (chèvre)

4   large whole wheat or white pita bread rounds, halved crosswise

Lettuce leaves

Clean mushrooms; cut off stems even with caps. Discard stems. Rinse mushroom caps. In a small bowl combine vinegar, oil, salt, and pepper; mix well. Brush mushrooms and sweet pepper quarters lightly with half of the oil mixture. If desired, place mushrooms and sweet peppers in a grill basket. Grill mushrooms and sweet peppers on the rack of an uncovered grill directly over medium coals for 10 to 12 minutes or until the vegetables are tender, turning occasionally.

Meanwhile, in a medium bowl combine remaining oil mixture, tomatoes, cucumber, and cheese; toss lightly to coat. Cut grilled mushrooms into ½-inch pieces. Cut sweet peppers into thin bite-size strips. Add mushrooms and sweet peppers to tomato mixture. Toss lightly to combine. Line pita bread with lettuce. Using a slotted spoon, fill pita halves with grilled vegetable mixture. Serve immediately. Makes 4 servings.

Great for outdoor dining, these pitas hold grilled vegetables and tangy feta cheese. A platter of fruit rounds out the meal.

grilled vegetable pitas

roasted vegetable pizzas

A light coating of olive oil nonstick cooking spray flavors this sauceless pizza while controlling the fat.

3 medium red, yellow, and/or green sweet peppers

1 medium onion, cut into very thin wedges and separated into strips

Olive oil nonstick cooking spray

1 16-ounce loaf frozen whole wheat bread dough, thawed

½ teaspoon crushed red pepper

1 cup shredded part-skim mozzarella cheese (4 ounces)

1 large red or yellow tomato, chopped

1 cup queso fresco or feta cheese (4 ounces)

2 tablespoons snipped fresh basil or oregano

Halve sweet peppers, removing stems, membranes, and seeds. Place peppers, cut sides down, on a baking sheet lined with foil. Lightly coat onion strips with nonstick cooking spray. Place onion strips around peppers. Bake in a 425° oven for 10 minutes. Remove onions and set aside. Bake peppers for 10 to 15 minutes more or until skin is bubbly and browned. Wrap peppers in the foil; let stand for 15 to 20 minutes or until cool enough to handle. Using a paring knife, gently pull off the skin. Cut peppers into 1-inch-wide strips.

Meanwhile, lightly coat two 12-inch pizza pans with nonstick cooking spray. Divide bread dough in half. Pat half of the dough into an 11-inch circle in each pizza pan, building up edges slightly. Prick bottom of crust with a fork. Do not let rise. Bake in a 425° oven about 10 minutes or until browned. Remove from oven; cool on wire racks.

Lightly coat each crust with nonstick cooking spray; sprinkle with crushed red pepper. Top with mozzarella cheese, roasted peppers, roasted onion, and tomato. Sprinkle with queso fresco or feta cheese.

Bake in a 425° oven about 7 minutes or until cheese is melted and crusts are crisp. Sprinkle with basil or oregano. Makes 8 servings.

Nutrition Facts per serving: 252 cal., 9 g total fat (1 g sat. fat), 21 mg chol., 474 mg sodium, 32 g carbo., 3 g fiber, 14 g pro. ▶ Exchanges: 2 Starch, ½ Vegetable, 1 Meat, ½ Fat

Nutrition Facts per serving: 269 cal., 7 g total fat (4 g sat. fat), 20 mg chol., 453 mg sodium, 38 g carbo., 1 g fiber, 12 g pro. ▶ Exchanges: 2 Starch, 1 Vegetable, ½ Meat, 1 Fat

1 small **zucchini, thinly sliced**

1 small **yellow summer squash, thinly sliced**

1 medium **onion, thinly sliced**

⅓ cup **sliced fresh mushrooms**

½ of a **red sweet pepper, cut into thin strips**

Olive oil nonstick cooking spray

Salt and black pepper

4 **pita bread rounds**

4 teaspoons **bottled vinaigrette or Italian salad dressing**

¾ cup **shredded Swiss cheese (3 ounces)**

Place zucchini, summer squash, onion, mushrooms, and sweet pepper on a baking sheet; lightly coat with nonstick cooking spray. Roast in a 450° oven about 10 minutes or until vegetables are tender. Season to taste with salt and pepper.

Divide roasted vegetables among pita bread rounds; drizzle with salad dressing. Top with shredded cheese. Place pitas on the unheated rack of a broiler pan. Broil 4 inches from heat about 3 minutes or until cheese melts. Makes 4 servings.

Cheese Storage Tips: To keep cheese fresh, leave it in the rind if it has one. Wrap unused cheese tightly in foil or plastic wrap; seal in a plastic bag or an airtight container. Store in the refrigerator. The softer the cheese, the shorter the storage life. Harder cheeses, such as sharp cheddar or Parmesan, will last for weeks in the refrigerator if properly stored.

Turn a modest Swiss cheese sandwich into a regal treat. Roast the vegetables while you relax.

roasted veggie and swiss sandwiches

open-face portobello sandwiches

Broiled or grilled, the portobello mushroom adds substance to this no-meat sandwich.

In a small bowl combine tomato, basil, thyme, and/or oregano, and salt; set aside. Cut the mushroom stems even with the caps; discard stems. Rinse mushroom caps; gently pat dry.

Combine vinegar and oil; gently brush over the mushrooms. Place mushrooms on the unheated rack of a broiler pan. Broil 4 to 5 inches from the heat for 6 to 8 minutes or until mushrooms are just tender, turning once halfway through broiling. (Or, grill mushrooms on the rack of an uncovered grill directly over medium coals for 6 to 8 minutes or until mushrooms are just tender, turning once halfway through grilling.) Drain mushrooms on paper towels; thinly slice mushrooms.

Place bread on a baking sheet. Broil for 2 to 3 minutes or until heated through.

To serve, top bread with mushrooms and tomato mixture. If desired, sprinkle with Parmesan cheese. Makes 4 servings.

⅔ cup chopped tomato

2 teaspoons snipped fresh basil, thyme, and/or oregano

⅛ teaspoon salt

2 medium fresh portobello mushrooms (about 4 inches in diameter)

1 teaspoon balsamic vinegar or red wine vinegar

½ teaspoon olive oil

½ of a 12-inch Italian flat bread (focaccia), quartered, or ½ of a 12-inch thin-crust Italian bread shell (Boboli)

Finely shredded Parmesan cheese (optional)

Nutrition Facts per serving: 161 cal., 3 g total fat (1 g sat. fat), 2 mg chol., 71 mg sodium, 29 g carbo., 3 g fiber, 7 g pro. ▶ Exchanges: 1½ Starch, 1½ Vegetable

113

12 ounces dried rotini, penne, or ziti

1 12-ounce package light firm tofu (fresh bean curd), drained

¼ cup oil-packed dried tomatoes, drained

¼ cup chicken broth

1 teaspoon dried oregano

1 teaspoon dried basil

1 to 2 chipotle peppers in adobo sauce

2 cloves garlic, minced

½ teaspoon salt

Finely shredded fresh basil leaves (optional)

Shaved Parmesan cheese (optional)

Cherry tomatoes, quartered (optional)

Cook the pasta according to package directions. Drain well; return pasta to pan and keep warm.

Meanwhile, in a blender container or food processor bowl combine tofu, dried tomatoes, broth, oregano, basil, chipotle peppers, garlic, and salt. Cover and blend or process until nearly smooth. Toss with hot cooked pasta; heat through. If desired, garnish with basil leaves, Parmesan cheese, and cherry tomatoes. Serve immediately. Makes 6 servings.

crimson pastatoss

Light tofu steps in for cream in this dried-tomato-and-chipotle-chile pasta sauce. Pureed tofu has a creamy texture and is rich in nutrients.

herbedpasta primavera

Combine the flavors of Italy with the cooking techniques of China.
Stir-fried vegetables keep their crisp freshness for the Italian sauce.

Cook pasta according to package directions; drain and keep warm. Meanwhile, for sauce, in a bowl stir together the 1 cup water, cornstarch, and bouillon granules; set aside.

Lightly coat a cold wok or large skillet with nonstick cooking spray. Heat over medium heat. Stir-fry carrots, green beans, leeks, basil, dill, and garlic for 4 minutes. Stir in yellow summer squash and the 2 tablespoons water. Cook, covered, for 4 to 5 minutes more or until the vegetables are crisp-tender. Remove vegetables from wok.

Stir sauce; add to wok. Cook and stir until thickened and bubbly. Cook and stir for 1 minute more. Return vegetables to wok; toss to coat. Heat through.

To serve, spoon vegetable mixture over hot pasta. Sprinkle with almonds and pepper. Makes 4 servings.

6 ounces **dried fusilli, fettuccine, or linguine**

1 cup **water**

2 teaspoons **cornstarch**

2 teaspoons **instant vegetable bouillon granules**

Nonstick cooking spray

3 medium **carrots, cut into thin bite-size pieces**

1½ cups **green beans bias-sliced into 2-inch pieces**

2 medium **leeks, cut into ¼-inch slices (⅔ cup)**

1 tablespoon **snipped fresh basil or ½ teaspoon dried basil, crushed**

1 tablespoon **snipped fresh dill or ½ teaspoon dried dillweed**

1 clove **garlic, minced**

1 medium **yellow summer squash, cut into thin bite-size pieces (1½ cups)**

2 tablespoons **water**

¼ cup **sliced almonds, toasted**

¼ teaspoon **coarsely ground black pepper**

Nutrition Facts per serving: 282 cal., 5 g total fat (0 g sat. fat), 0 mg chol., 478 mg sodium, 53 g carbo., 7 g fiber, 10 g pro. ▶ Exchanges: 2½ Starch, 2½ Vegetable, ½ Fat

Nutrition Facts per serving: 368 cal., 8 g total fat (1 g sat. fat), 12 mg chol., 393 mg sodium, 57 g carbo., 6 g fiber, 19 g pro. ▶ Exchanges: 3 Starch, 1½ Vegetable, 1 Meat, ½ F

8 ounces dried penne or ziti

2½ cups fresh broccoli flowerets

1½ cups 1-inch pieces fresh asparagus or green beans

2 large ripe tomatoes

1 cup light ricotta cheese

¼ cup shredded fresh basil

4 teaspoons snipped fresh thyme

4 teaspoons balsamic vinegar

1 tablespoon olive oil

1 clove garlic, minced

½ teaspoon salt

½ teaspoon freshly ground black pepper

2 tablespoons grated Parmesan or Romano cheese

Fresh thyme (optional)

Cook pasta according to package directions, adding broccoli and asparagus or beans during the last 3 minutes of cooking.

Meanwhile, place a fine strainer over a large bowl. Cut tomatoes in half; squeeze seeds and juice into strainer. With the back of a spoon, press seeds to extract juice; discard seeds. Add ricotta cheese, basil, thyme, vinegar, oil, garlic, salt, and pepper to tomato juice; mix well. Chop tomatoes; stir into ricotta mixture.

Drain pasta and vegetables; add to bowl and toss well. Sprinkle with Parmesan or Romano cheese. If desired, garnish with thyme. Makes 4 servings.

Eating enough vegetables throughout the day is easy when you feature this bouquet of veggies over pasta.

pasta with ricotta and vegetables

deli-style pasta salad

A zesty fresh herb-and-Dijon-mustard vinaigrette lightens up this picnic-perfect pasta salad.

½ of a 16-ounce package (about 2 cups) frozen cheese-filled tortellini or one 9-ounce package refrigerated cheese-filled tortellini

1½ cups broccoli flowerets

1 large carrot, thinly sliced (¾ cup)

1 medium red or yellow sweet pepper, chopped (¾ cup)

¼ cup white wine vinegar

2 tablespoons olive oil

1 teaspoon dried Italian seasoning, crushed

1 teaspoon Dijon-style mustard

¼ teaspoon black pepper

⅛ teaspoon garlic powder

Kale leaves (optional)

In a large saucepan cook pasta according to package directions, omitting salt and oil. Add the broccoli, carrot, and sweet pepper to pasta during the last 3 minutes of cooking. Drain. Rinse with cold water; drain again.

For dressing, in a screw-top jar combine the vinegar, olive oil, Italian seasoning, mustard, pepper, and garlic powder. Cover and shake well.

Pour dressing over pasta mixture; toss gently to coat. Stir mixture before serving. If desired, line serving bowl with kale leaves. Makes 4 servings.

TAKE A DEEP BREATH ▶ MIND·BODY·SPIRIT

When you're feeling rattled, pay attention to your breathing. Short, shallow breathing often accompanies stress. Slow, deep breathing counters the "fight or flight" state so you can think clearly and relax. To remain calm in a stressful situation, take a deep breath through your nose, pressing your abdomen out. Hold the breath for a count of five. Slowly exhale through your mouth, pulling your abdomen in. Do this cycle at least five times for the most benefit.

Nutrition Facts per serving: 305 cal., 12 g total fat (2 g sat. fat), 30 mg chol., 315 mg sodium, 41 g carbo., 4 g fiber, 13 g pro. ▶ Exchanges: 2 Starch, 1 Vegetable, 1 Meat, 1½ Fat

Nutrition Facts per serving: 370 cal., 6 g total fat (1 g sat. fat), 2 mg chol., 262 mg sodium, 65 g carbo., 9 g fiber, 17 g pro. ▶ Exchanges: 3½ Starch, 2 Vegetable, ½ Meat, ½ Fat

6 ounces **dried fettuccine**

1 tablespoon **olive oil**

Nonstick cooking spray

1 9-ounce package **frozen artichoke hearts, thawed, or one 14-ounce can or jar artichoke hearts, rinsed and drained**

2 medium **red and/or green sweet peppers, chopped (1½ cups)**

⅓ cup **finely chopped onion**

2 cloves **garlic, minced**

1 15-ounce can **Great Northern beans, drained and rinsed**

2 medium **tomatoes, chopped (1½ cups)**

1 tablespoon **snipped fresh basil or 1 teaspoon dried basil, crushed**

Black pepper

2 tablespoons **grated Parmesan cheese**

Cook pasta according to package directions. Drain; return to saucepan. Toss with olive oil; keep warm.

Meanwhile, lightly coat a large skillet with nonstick cooking spray. Heat over medium heat. Cut up any large pieces of artichoke. Add artichokes, sweet peppers, onion, and garlic to skillet; cook and stir for 5 to 6 minutes or until vegetables are tender. Stir in beans, tomatoes, and basil; heat through.

Add vegetable mixture to pasta; toss gently to combine. Season to taste with pepper. Sprinkle each serving with Parmesan cheese. Makes 4 servings.

Simple beans and pasta are distinguished dinner fare with the addition of fresh basil, tomatoes, and artichokes.

pasta and beans with artichokes

asian vegetable lo mein

Udon noodles are usually sold in the Asian food section of the supermarket. If unavailable, substitute spaghetti or linguine.

In a small bowl combine mushrooms and boiling water. Cover and let stand for 20 minutes. Drain mushrooms, squeezing out excess liquid; reserve ½ cup liquid. Chop mushrooms and set aside. Meanwhile, cook noodles in additional boiling water for 5 minutes; drain and return to saucepan.

For egg strips, combine egg whites and egg. In a 10-inch nonstick skillet heat 1 teaspoon of the cooking oil and 1 teaspoon of the sesame oil over medium heat until hot. Pour egg mixture into skillet. Lift and tilt the skillet to form a thin layer of egg on the bottom. Cook, without stirring, for 2 or 3 minutes or until just set. Slide egg mixture out onto a cutting board; cool slightly and cut into 2×½-inch strips. Set aside.

In the same skillet heat remaining 1 teaspoon cooking oil and 1 teaspoon sesame oil over medium-high heat. Add mushrooms, garlic, ginger, and, if desired, crushed red pepper. Cook and stir for 1 minute. Add sweet pepper and peas; cook and stir for 2 minutes more. Add reserved mushroom soaking liquid and teriyaki sauce. Bring to boiling; boil gently, uncovered, for 3 minutes. Add egg strips and vegetable mixture to noodles; toss well. Serve immediately. Makes 4 servings.

1 cup dried shiitake or Chinese black mushrooms

1 cup boiling water

6 ounces udon noodles

2 egg whites

1 egg

2 teaspoons cooking oil

2 teaspoons toasted sesame oil

3 cloves garlic, minced

2 teaspoons finely chopped fresh ginger

½ teaspoon crushed red pepper (optional)

1 red sweet pepper, cut into thin bite-size strips

2 cups sugar snap peas or snow pea pods (strings and tips removed), halved

¼ cup light teriyaki sauce

Nutrition Facts per serving: 293 cal., 8 g total fat (1 g sat. fat), 94 mg chol., 307 mg sodium, 44 g carbo., 3 g fiber, 12 g pro. ▶ Exchanges: 2½ Starch, 1 Vegetable, ½ Meat, 1 Fat

pasta with red pepper sauce

Wickedly delicious sweet red pepper sauce tops pasta in this meat-free entrée. Serve it with a crisp green salad.

6 medium red sweet peppers, chopped, or two 12-ounce jars roasted red sweet peppers, drained

4 cloves garlic

2 tablespoons olive oil

1 cup water

⅔ cup loosely packed snipped fresh basil or 2 tablespoons dried basil, crushed

½ cup tomato paste

2 tablespoons red wine vinegar

8 ounces hot cooked pasta, such as penne, cavatelli, or tortellini

Grated Parmesan cheese (optional)

For sauce, in a large skillet cook sweet peppers and garlic in oil over medium heat about 20 minutes, stirring occasionally. (Or, if using peppers from a jar, in a 2-quart saucepan cook garlic in hot oil for 3 to 4 minutes or until light brown.)

Place half of the pepper-garlic mixture in a blender container or food processor bowl. Cover; blend or process until nearly smooth. Add half each of the water, basil, tomato paste, and vinegar. Cover and blend or process with several on-and-off turns until basil is just chopped and mixture is nearly smooth. Transfer pepper mixture to a 2-quart saucepan. Repeat with remaining peppers, water, basil, tomato paste, and vinegar; transfer to the saucepan.

Cook and stir sauce over medium heat until heated through. Serve sauce over pasta. If desired, sprinkle with Parmesan cheese. Makes 4 servings.

Nutrition Facts per serving: 332 cal., 8 g total fat (1 g sat. fat), 0 mg chol., 48 mg sodium, 57 g carbo., 3 g fiber, 10 g pro. ▶ Exchanges: 3 Starch, 2 Vegetable, 1 Fat

1 9-ounce package refrigerated cheese-filled tortellini

1 9-ounce package frozen artichoke hearts

½ of a 6-ounce package (about 1 cup) frozen pea pods

1 7-ounce jar roasted red sweet peppers, drained and cut into thin strips

½ of an 8-ounce package reduced-fat cream cheese (Neufchâtel) or fat-free cheese, cut up

1 cup evaporated fat-free milk

⅛ teaspoon salt

⅛ teaspoon black pepper

¼ cup grated Parmesan cheese

In a 4-quart Dutch oven bring a large amount of water to boiling. Add tortellini and artichoke hearts; return to boiling. Reduce heat and cook, uncovered, for 6 minutes. Add pea pods; continue cooking about 1 minute more or until pasta and vegetables are tender. Drain. Stir in sweet pepper strips; keep warm.

Meanwhile, for sauce, in a medium saucepan combine cream cheese, milk, salt, and pepper. Cook and stir over medium heat until slightly thickened and smooth.

Pour the sauce over the pasta mixture. Sprinkle with 2 tablespoons of the Parmesan cheese; toss gently to coat pasta and vegetables with sauce. Sprinkle with remaining Parmesan cheese. Makes 4 servings.

No chopping or dicing required. Assemble and cook with little mess or effort for this pasta dish.

tortellini with creamy vegetables

spinach and cheese roll-ups

For ease, use purchased spaghetti or marinara sauce instead of making the homemade sauce.

For sauce, in a medium saucepan cook onion and garlic in hot oil until onion is tender, stirring occasionally. Carefully stir in undrained tomatoes, tomato paste, basil, sugar, salt, and pepper. Bring to boiling; reduce heat. Simmer, uncovered, about 5 minutes or until sauce is desired consistency, stirring occasionally.

Meanwhile, cook pasta according to package directions; drain. Rinse with cold water; drain well.

For filling, drain thawed spinach well, pressing out excess liquid. In a medium bowl stir together ricotta cheese, mozzarella cheese, Parmesan cheese, and basil. Add spinach and egg white, stirring to combine.

To assemble, evenly spread about ¼ cup filling on each noodle. Roll up from one end. Place two rolls, seam side down, into each of four individual casseroles. Top each serving with sauce.

Bake casseroles, covered, in a 350° oven about 25 minutes or until heated through. Makes 4 servings.

⅓ cup chopped onion

1 clove garlic, minced

1 teaspoon olive oil or cooking oil

1 14½-ounce can tomatoes, cut up

2 tablespoons tomato paste

1½ teaspoons snipped fresh basil or ½ teaspoon dried basil, crushed

¼ teaspoon sugar

Dash salt

Dash black pepper

8 dried lasagna noodles

1 10-ounce package frozen chopped spinach, thawed

¾ cup fat-free or reduced-fat ricotta cheese

½ cup shredded part-skim mozzarella cheese (2 ounces)

2 tablespoons finely shredded Parmesan cheese

2 teaspoons snipped fresh basil or ½ teaspoon dried basil or Italian seasoning, crushed

1 slightly beaten egg white

Nutrition Facts per serving: 231 cal., 3 g total fat (0 g sat. fat), 10 mg chol., 425 mg sodium, 39 g carbo., 2 g fiber, 20 g pro. ▶ Exchanges: 1½ Starch, 2 Vegetable, 1½ Meat

broccoli with ginger tofu

Enjoy an iron-rich meatless meal when you serve this dish of rice, broccoli, tofu, and cashews.

1 cup short-grain rice

2 stalks fresh broccoli (12 ounces)

⅓ cup reduced-sodium chicken broth

3 tablespoons reduced-sodium soy sauce

1 tablespoon dry sherry

1 tablespoon grated fresh ginger

2 teaspoons cornstarch

1 tablespoon peanut oil

4 cloves garlic, minced

1 medium red sweet pepper, cut into thin bite-size strips

8 ounces extra-firm tofu (fresh bean curd), drained and cut into ½-inch cubes

2 tablespoons coarsely chopped cashews

Cook rice according to package directions; keep warm.

Remove flowerets from broccoli stalks and cut, as necessary, into smaller flowerets. Peel broccoli stems; cut crosswise into thin rounds. Set broccoli aside. (You should have 4 to 4½ cups.)

In a small bowl combine the chicken broth, soy sauce, sherry, ginger, and cornstarch. Set aside.

Pour peanut oil into a large skillet or wok. Preheat over medium-high heat. Stir-fry garlic in hot oil for 30 seconds. Add broccoli and sweet pepper; stir-fry for 4 to 5 minutes or until vegetables are crisp-tender. Push vegetables to the side of skillet. Stir chicken broth mixture; add to the center of skillet. Cook and stir until thickened and bubbly. Gently stir in tofu. Cook and stir for 1 to 2 minutes more or until heated through. Serve over rice; sprinkle with cashews. Makes 4 to 5 servings.

Nutrition Facts per serving: 364 cal., 11 g total fat (2 g sat. fat), 0 mg chol., 482 mg sodium, 51 g carbo., 4 g fiber, 17 g pro. ▶ Exchanges: 3 Starch, 1 Vegetable, ½ Meat, 1 Fat

Nutrition Facts per serving: 203 cal., 9 g total fat (4 g sat. fat), 23 mg chol., 320 mg sodium, 21 g carbo., 1 g fiber, 12 g pro. ▶ Exchanges: 1 Starch, 1 Vegetable, 1 Meat, 1 Fat

Cook pasta according to package directions; drain and set aside.

Meanwhile, for filling, drain thawed spinach well, pressing out excess liquid. In a medium bowl combine spinach, feta cheese, ricotta cheese, walnuts, egg white, cinnamon, and pepper; set aside.

For sauce, combine undrained tomatoes, tomato paste, mint, sugar, and garlic. Stuff each pasta shell with 2 slightly rounded tablespoons of the spinach filling. Arrange filled pasta shells in an ungreased 2-quart square baking dish. Spoon sauce over shells. Bake, covered, in a 350° oven for 30 to 35 minutes or until heated through. Sprinkle with mozzarella cheese. Bake, uncovered, for 2 to 3 minutes more or until cheese is melted. Makes 6 servings.

baked
spinach-feta shells

12 dried jumbo pasta shells

1 10-ounce package frozen chopped spinach, thawed and well drained

½ cup crumbled feta cheese (about 2 ounces)

½ cup fat-free ricotta cheese

¼ cup chopped walnuts, toasted

1 slightly beaten egg white

⅛ teaspoon ground cinnamon

⅛ teaspoon black pepper

1 14½-ounce can low-sodium tomatoes, undrained and cut up

2 tablespoons reduced-sodium tomato paste

1 tablespoon snipped fresh mint or 1 teaspoon dried mint, crushed

1 teaspoon sugar

1 clove garlic, minced, or ¼ teaspoon garlic powder

¼ cup shredded reduced-fat mozzarella cheese

Use mint instead of salt to bring refreshing flavor to sauces. Or try another herb next time. Cooking your own meals gives you versatility.

Nutrition Facts per serving: 198 cal., 10 g total fat (1 g sat. fat), 0 mg chol., 410 mg sodium, 14 g carbo., 3 g fiber, 16 g pro. ▶ Exchanges: ½ Starch, 1½ Vegetable, 1 Meat, 1 F

1 10½-ounce package light extra-firm tofu (fresh bean curd), drained

3 tablespoons reduced-sodium tamari or soy sauce

8 green onions

8 ounces snow pea pods (2 cups), strings and tips removed

1 tablespoon toasted sesame oil

1 red sweet pepper, cut into long, thin strips

1 yellow sweet pepper, cut into long, thin strips

2 tablespoons cornmeal

1 tablespoon white or black sesame seed, toasted (optional)

Cut tofu crosswise into 8 slices. Arrange slices in one layer on a large plate or jelly-roll pan. Pour tamari or soy sauce over tofu; turn slices to coat and let stand for 1 hour.

Meanwhile, cut root ends off green onions. Cut off dark green portion of onions, leaving 3 inches of white and light green. Cut green onions in half lengthwise, forming 16 long strips. Set aside. Cut pea pods in half lengthwise. Set aside.

Pour oil into a large nonstick skillet. Preheat over medium-high heat. Stir-fry sweet pepper strips for 1 minute. Add green onions and pea pods; stir-fry for 2 to 3 minutes more or until crisp-tender.

Drain tofu, reserving tamari or soy sauce. Stir reserved tamari or soy sauce into cooked vegetables; transfer vegetable mixture to a serving platter. Cover and keep warm. Carefully dip tofu slices in cornmeal to lightly coat both sides. Cook in same skillet for 3 minutes on each side or until crisp and hot, using a spatula to turn carefully. (You may need to cook tofu slices in two batches; do not crowd the skillet.) Serve tofu slices with vegetables. If desired, sprinkle with sesame seed. Makes 4 servings.

The contrast of the crispy, crunchy coating and silken interior of these tofu cutlets may convert the most avowed meat-lover.

crispy tofu and vegetables

1⅓ cups water

½ cup dry lentils, rinsed and drained

8 6- or 7-inch flour tortillas

Nonstick cooking spray

2 medium carrots, thinly sliced (1 cup)

1 medium zucchini or yellow summer squash, quartered lengthwise and sliced (2 cups)

2 teaspoons chili powder or 1 teaspoon ground cumin

1 14½-ounce can chunky Mexican-style stewed tomatoes

1 cup shredded reduced-fat Monterey Jack cheese (4 ounces)

¼ teaspoon salt

Dash bottled hot pepper sauce (optional)

In a medium saucepan combine water and drained lentils. Bring to boiling; reduce heat. Simmer, covered, for 15 to 20 minutes or until tender. Drain lentils; set aside.

Meanwhile, wrap tortillas tightly in foil. Heat in a 350° oven for 10 minutes to soften. Lightly coat a 2-quart rectangular baking dish with nonstick cooking spray; set aside.

Lightly coat a large cold skillet with nonstick cooking spray. Heat over medium heat. Stir-fry the carrots for 2 minutes. Add zucchini or summer squash and chili powder or cumin; stir-fry for 2 to 3 minutes or until vegetables are crisp-tender. Remove skillet from heat. Stir in lentils, half of the undrained stewed tomatoes, ¾ cup of the cheese, salt, and, if desired, the hot pepper sauce.

Divide vegetable mixture evenly among warm tortillas; roll up tortillas. Arrange tortillas, seam side down, in prepared baking dish. Lightly coat tops of tortillas with nonstick cooking spray. Bake, uncovered, in a 350° oven for 12 to 15 minutes or until heated through and tortillas are crisp.

Meanwhile, in a saucepan heat remaining undrained tomatoes. Spoon over enchiladas; top with remaining cheese. Makes 4 servings.

Lentils and fresh vegetables wrapped in tortillas make these enchiladas a meal unto themselves.

spicy vegetable enchiladas

vegetable-topped couscous

Couscous is a great item to have on your shelf. It cooks in 5 minutes and can often take the place of a side of steamed rice.

In a large saucepan cook onion and garlic in hot oil over medium-low heat until onion is crisp-tender. Stir in carrots, the ½ cup water, basil, cumin, salt, and, if desired, red pepper. Bring to boiling; reduce heat. Simmer, covered, for 10 minutes.

Stir in zucchini, garbanzo beans, and undrained tomatoes. Cook, covered, for 2 minutes. Stir together the 2 tablespoons cold water and cornstarch; stir into tomato mixture. Cook and stir until thickened and bubbly. Cook and stir for 2 minutes more.

Meanwhile, in a medium saucepan bring chicken broth to boiling. Remove saucepan from heat. Stir in couscous. Cover and let stand for 5 minutes or until liquid is absorbed; fluff with a fork. Serve vegetable mixture over couscous. Sprinkle with peanuts. Makes 4 servings.

1 large onion, cut into thin wedges

2 cloves garlic, minced

1 teaspoon olive oil or cooking oil

2 cups thinly sliced carrots

½ cup water

1 teaspoon dried basil, crushed

½ teaspoon ground cumin

¼ teaspoon salt

⅛ teaspoon ground red pepper (optional)

2 medium zucchini, quartered lengthwise and cut into ½-inch pieces (2½ cups)

1 15-ounce can garbanzo beans, drained and rinsed

1 14½-ounce can low-sodium stewed tomatoes

2 tablespoons cold water

2 teaspoons cornstarch

2 cups reduced-sodium chicken broth

1 cup quick-cooking couscous

¼ cup chopped, unsalted dry-roasted peanuts

Nutrition Facts per serving: 423 cal., 8 g total fat (1 g sat. fat), 0 mg chol., 892 mg sodium, 73 g carbo., 17 g fiber, 16 g pro. ▶ Exchanges: 4 Starch, 2 Vegetable, ½ Meat, 1 Fat

Nutrition Facts per serving: 260 cal., 8 g total fat (1 g sat. fat), 9 mg chol., 576 mg sodium, 38 g carbo., 5 g fiber, 10 g pro. ▶ Exchanges: 2 Starch, 1 Vegetable, 1 Fat

1 16-ounce package refrigerated cooked polenta

1 small **green sweet pepper**, seeded and cut into thin strips

1 small **onion**, thinly sliced

1 clove **garlic**, minced

1 tablespoon **cooking oil**

½ small **eggplant**, cut into ½-inch pieces

1 large **yellow summer squash** or **zucchini**, sliced

1 large **tomato**, cut into wedges

1 cup small **pattypan squash**, quartered

1 tablespoon snipped fresh **basil**

⅛ teaspoon **salt**

⅛ teaspoon **black pepper**

3 tablespoons snipped fresh **parsley**

Shredded Parmesan cheese (optional)

Prepare purchased polenta according to package directions. Cover and keep warm.

For ratatouille, in a 4-quart saucepan cook sweet pepper, onion, and garlic in hot oil over medium heat for 5 minutes, stirring frequently. Add the eggplant; cook for 5 minutes more, stirring frequently. Stir in summer squash or zucchini, tomato, pattypan squash, basil, salt, and pepper. Cook, covered, for 5 to 7 minutes more or until vegetables are tender, stirring occasionally. Stir in parsley.

To serve, cut polenta into 8 to 12 slices. Place 2 slices of polenta on 4 to 6 dinner plates. Spoon warm ratatouille over each serving. If desired, sprinkle with Parmesan cheese. Makes 4 to 6 servings.

Purchased polenta complements this entrée. Look for it in the produce section of your supermarket or with the refrigerated tortillas.

ratatouille over polenta

Nutrition Facts per serving: 197 cal., 6 g total fat (2 g sat. fat), 11 mg chol., 401 mg sodium, 23 g carbo., 3 g fiber, 13 g pro. ▶ Exchanges: 1½ Starch, 1½ Meat, ½ Fat

1 cup refrigerated or frozen egg product, thawed

¼ cup chopped onion

¼ cup grated Parmesan cheese

½ of a 20-ounce package refrigerated shredded hash brown potatoes (about 3 cups)

2 medium zucchini, thinly sliced (2½ cups)

1 clove garlic, minced

1 teaspoon cooking oil

3 ounces sliced reduced-fat Swiss cheese

¼ cup fat-free milk

2 teaspoons snipped fresh oregano or ½ teaspoon dried oregano, crushed

¼ teaspoon black pepper

⅛ teaspoon salt

In a large bowl combine ¼ cup of the egg product, onion, and Parmesan cheese. Stir in potatoes. Transfer mixture to a greased 9-inch pie plate; pat mixture into the bottom and up the sides.

Bake, uncovered, in a 400° oven for 35 to 40 minutes or until golden. Cool slightly on a wire rack. Reduce oven temperature to 350°.

In a large skillet cook zucchini and garlic in hot oil until zucchini is crisp-tender; cool slightly. Place cheese slices in bottom of crust, tearing to fit. Arrange zucchini mixture over cheese.

In a small bowl combine the remaining ¾ cup egg product, milk, oregano, pepper, and salt. Pour over the zucchini mixture in crust.

Bake in the 350° oven for 25 to 30 minutes or until filling appears set when gently shaken. Let stand for 10 minutes before serving. Makes 6 servings.

Use Parmesan cheese to flavor and enrich a hash brown potato crust. It's a delicious base for a vegetable-custard filling.

zucchini and swiss pie

roasted vegetables parmesan

Buy the best Parmesan cheese available and grate it over the roasted vegetables. You won't be disappointed.

In a large roasting pan combine zucchini, onion, sweet pepper, mushrooms, and carrots. Drizzle with oil; toss to coat. Spread vegetables evenly in roasting pan. Sprinkle with salt.

Roast zucchini mixture in a 500° oven for 12 minutes. Remove from oven; stir in beans and drained tomatoes. Reduce heat to 375°. Roast, uncovered, about 10 minutes more or until heated through. To serve, sprinkle with Parmesan cheese. Makes 6 servings.

2 medium **zucchini, cut into 1-inch pieces**

1 medium **onion, cut into 8 wedges**

1 medium **red or green sweet pepper, cut into 1-inch pieces**

8 ounces **fresh mushrooms, stems removed**

1 cup **packaged peeled baby carrots**

1 tablespoon **olive oil**

½ teaspoon **salt**

1 15-ounce can **garbanzo beans, drained and rinsed**

1 14½-ounce can **diced tomatoes with garlic and Italian herbs, drained**

½ cup **shredded Parmesan cheese**

MIND·BODY·SPIRIT ▶ ACT "AS IF"

When you're working toward a goal, one positive thing you can do is to act as if you've made it. Believing that you will obtain your desires is the first step in the process. Many athletes visualize an outcome, such as winning a race, before it actually happens. Do you want a new job? A healthy, loving relationship? First, believe that it will happen, visualize that it has happened, then take action to make it true. The outcome may amaze you.

Nutrition Facts per serving: 160 cal., 6 g total fat (0 g sat. fat), 7 mg chol., 867 mg sodium, 20 g carbo., 5 g fiber, 8 g pro. ▶ Exchanges: ½ Starch, 2½ Vegetable, 1 Fat

Nutrition Facts per serving: 254 cal., 5 g total fat (0 g sat. fat), 5 mg chol., 530 mg sodium, 44 g carbo., 5 g fiber, 12 g pro. ▶ Exchanges: 2½ Starch, 1½ Vegetable, ½ Fat

1 14½-ounce can vegetable broth

1 medium onion, chopped (½ cup)

½ cup dry lentils, drained and rinsed

½ cup long grain rice

¼ cup water

1 teaspoon finely shredded lemon peel

1½ cups small broccoli flowerets, sliced zucchini or summer squash, and/or pea pods

1 medium carrot, cut into thin strips (½ cup)

½ small eggplant, peeled and diced (2 cups)

2 cloves garlic, minced

2 teaspoons olive oil

3 plum tomatoes, chopped (1 cup)

¼ cup shredded fresh basil

¼ cup finely shredded Asiago or Parmesan cheese

In a 3-quart saucepan combine broth, onion, lentils, uncooked rice, water, and lemon peel. Bring to boiling; reduce heat. Simmer, covered, for 20 minutes, adding broccoli, zucchini or squash, and/or pea pods, and carrot during the last 3 to 5 minutes of cooking time.

Meanwhile, in a 10-inch skillet cook the eggplant and garlic in hot oil over medium heat until the eggplant is soft, about 10 minutes.

Remove lentil mixture from heat; let stand for 5 minutes. Carefully stir in eggplant mixture, tomatoes, and basil. To serve, sprinkle with cheese. Makes 4 servings.

The essences of lemon and fresh basil heighten the flavors of garden-fresh summer vegetables in this lentil and rice pilaf.

summer vegetable pilaf

Spaghetti squash got its name from the amazing strands that form after it is cooked. Use a fork to pull out the strands.

1 medium **spaghetti squash** (2½ to 3 pounds), halved and seeded

1 10-ounce package **frozen baby lima beans**

1 15-ounce can **red kidney beans**, drained and rinsed

½ of a 7-ounce jar (½ cup) **roasted red sweet peppers**, rinsed, drained, and cut into short strips

½ teaspoon **salt**

¼ cup **balsamic vinegar**

3 tablespoons **olive oil**

1 tablespoon **honey mustard**

2 cloves **garlic**, minced

Freshly ground **black pepper** (optional)

Place squash halves in a large Dutch oven with about 1 inch of water. Bring to boiling. Cook, covered, for 15 to 20 minutes or until tender.

Meanwhile, in a saucepan cook lima beans according to package directions, adding kidney beans during the last 3 minutes of cooking; drain and return to pan. Stir in roasted sweet peppers and salt; heat through.

For vinaigrette, in a screw-top jar combine vinegar, oil, honey mustard, and garlic. Cover; shake well. Pour vinaigrette over bean mixture; toss to coat.

Use a fork to scrape the strings of squash pulp from the shells, separating it into strands. Return strands to each shell. Spoon the warm bean mixture over the squash strands in shells, drizzling any excess vinaigrette on top. If desired, sprinkle with pepper. To serve, cut each squash shell in half. Makes 4 servings.

Nutrition Facts per serving: 421 cal., 11 g total fat (2 g sat. fat), 0 mg chol., 466 mg sodium, 65 g carbo., 13 g fiber, 21 g pro. ▶ Exchanges: 3½ Starch, 3 Vegetable, 1½ Fat

Nutrition Facts per serving: 337 cal., 10 g total fat (7 g sat. fat), 38 mg chol., 508 mg sodium, 49 g carbo., 6 g fiber, 13 g pro. ▶ Exchanges: 2½ Starch, 1½ Vegetable, 1 Meat, 1 Fat

1¾ cups **water**

¾ cup **brown rice**

⅓ cup **wild rice**

1 teaspoon **dried fines herbes or dried basil, crushed**

⅛ teaspoon **black pepper**

2 cups **bias-sliced carrots**

1 cup **halved baby zucchini**

2 cups **snow pea pods, strings and tips removed**

1 medium **tomato, cut into wedges**

⅔ cup **crumbled feta cheese**

For rice mixture, in a medium saucepan bring water to boiling. Stir in brown rice and wild rice; reduce heat. Simmer, covered, about 50 minutes or until rice is tender and liquid is absorbed. Stir fines herbes or basil and pepper into rice mixture; keep warm.

Meanwhile, place carrots in a steamer basket over simmering water. Cover and steam for 5 minutes. Add zucchini; steam for 3 minutes. Halve pea pods; add pea pods and tomato wedges to steamer basket. Steam, covered, for 2 to 3 minutes more or until vegetables are tender.

Spoon rice mixture onto a serving platter; top with steamed vegetables. Sprinkle with feta cheese. Cover platter with foil; let stand for 3 minutes before serving to soften cheese. Makes 4 servings.

steamedveggies withfeta

When you have a craving for vegetables, try this steamed veggie dish. It's served with brown rice and topped with feta.

CHAPTER FIVE

satisfyings

oups

Nutrition facts per serving: 246 cal., 9 g total fat (2 g sat. fat), 60 mg chol., 735 mg sodium, 14 g carbo., 3 g fiber, 26 g pro. ▶ Exchanges: ½ Starch, 1½ Vegetable, 3 Meat

1 large onion, finely chopped

4 cloves garlic, minced

1 tablespoon olive oil or cooking oil

12 ounces skinless, boneless chicken breast halves, cut into bite-size pieces

1 14½-ounce can chicken broth

2 teaspoons chopped canned chipotle peppers in adobo sauce

½ teaspoon sugar

¼ teaspoon salt

2 cups chopped tomatoes or one 14½-ounce can low-sodium diced tomatoes

¼ cup snipped fresh cilantro

In a Dutch oven cook the onion and garlic in hot oil over medium-high heat about 4 minutes or until onion is tender. Add the chicken; cook for 2 minutes. Stir in chicken broth, chipotle peppers, sugar, and salt.

Bring to boiling; reduce heat. Simmer, uncovered, for 15 minutes. Remove from heat. Stir in the tomatoes and cilantro. Makes 3 servings.

Chicken Tip: A 3-ounce uncooked serving of chicken breast with skin has about 144 calories and 8 grams fat.* Remove the skin and it drops to 92 calories and 1 gram fat.* Although keeping skin on during roasting keeps chicken moist it's more healthful to remove it before eating.

*Based on information from USDA Nutrient Database.

Add complex, smoky flavor to a chicken-and-tomato-based soup by stirring in a bit of chipotle chile, which is a smoked jalapeño.

chipotle chile pepper soup

hot and sour chicken soup

A satisfying soup doesn't have to take long to make.
This Chinese-style favorite takes less than 15 minutes to cook.

In a large saucepan heat oil over medium heat. Add mushrooms and garlic. Cook for 4 minutes, stirring occasionally. Stir in broth, vinegar, soy sauce, and red pepper or chili oil; bring to boiling. Stir in cole slaw mix or cabbage and cooked chicken; reduce heat. Simmer, uncovered, for 5 minutes.

Combine water and cornstarch, stirring until smooth; stir into soup. Bring to boiling. Cook about 2 minutes or until slightly thickened. Remove saucepan from heat; stir in sesame oil. Makes 4 servings.

2 teaspoons peanut oil or cooking oil

4 ounces sliced fresh shiitake mushrooms

2 cloves garlic, minced

2 14½-ounce cans reduced-sodium chicken broth

2 tablespoons white vinegar or rice vinegar

2 tablespoons reduced-sodium soy sauce

½ teaspoon crushed red pepper or 1 teaspoon chili oil

2 cups packaged shredded cabbage with carrot (cole slaw mix) or shredded Chinese cabbage

1 cup shredded cooked chicken

2 tablespoons water

1 tablespoon cornstarch

1 teaspoon toasted sesame oil

MIND·BODY·SPIRIT ▶ TAKE TIME FOR TEA

An afternoon tea break is refreshing, healthful, and may help in weight loss. Green tea contains polyphenols or catechins, which are antioxidants called tannins. These compounds appear to help guard against cancer and lower the risk of heart disease. Another benefit for those trying to drop the pounds is that green tea extract (in pill form) has been shown to boost metabolism.

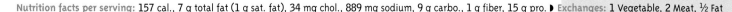

Nutrition facts per serving: 157 cal., 7 g total fat (1 g sat. fat), 34 mg chol., 889 mg sodium, 9 g carbo., 1 g fiber, 15 g pro. ▶ Exchanges: 1 Vegetable, 2 Meat, ½ Fat

moroccan chicken stew

Aromatic cumin, paprika, cinnamon, and saffron give this chicken and vegetable stew a full-bodied taste in a short cooking time.

Cook couscous according to package directions, except omit oil and salt; keep warm.

Meanwhile, in a large nonstick skillet heat oil over medium-high heat. Add chicken, shallots, and garlic to skillet. Cook for 2 minutes, stirring occasionally.

In a small bowl combine salt, paprika, cumin, cinnamon, saffron or turmeric, and ground red pepper; sprinkle evenly over chicken mixture in skillet. Cook and stir for 2 minutes more or until chicken is tender and no longer pink.

Cut any large pieces of squash or zucchini and carrots in half; add to skillet along with broth and raisins. Bring to boiling. Simmer, covered, for 6 to 8 minutes or until vegetables are crisp-tender. Serve stew over couscous. If desired, garnish with fresh mint. Makes 4 servings.

1 cup **quick-cooking couscous**

1 tablespoon **olive oil**

12 ounces **skinless, boneless chicken thighs or breast halves, cut into 1-inch pieces**

⅓ cup **sliced shallots**

3 cloves **garlic, minced**

½ teaspoon **salt**

½ teaspoon **paprika**

½ teaspoon **ground cumin**

¼ teaspoon **ground cinnamon**

¼ teaspoon **ground saffron or ground turmeric**

⅛ teaspoon **ground red pepper**

6 ounces **baby pattypan squash or 1½ cups sliced zucchini**

1 cup **slender baby carrots, tops trimmed, or packaged peeled baby carrots**

1 cup **reduced-sodium chicken broth**

¼ cup **golden or dark raisins**

Fresh mint (optional)

Nutrition Facts per serving: 363 cal., 7 g total fat (1 g sat. fat), 45 mg chol., 496 mg sodium, 51 g carbo., 9 g fiber, 24 g pro. ▶ Exchanges: 2½ Starch, 1 Vegetable, ½ Fruit, 2 Meat

turkey and mushroom soup

The favorite part of roasting a turkey might be knowing you can have this soup the next day.

2 cups sliced fresh mushrooms (such as cremini, shiitake, porcini, or button)

1 stalk celery, thinly sliced

1 medium carrot, thinly sliced

1 small onion, chopped

1 tablespoon margarine or butter

4½ cups water

1 tablespoon instant beef bouillon granules

⅛ teaspoon black pepper

½ cup dried orzo (rosamarina)

1½ cups chopped cooked turkey

2 tablespoons snipped fresh parsley

1 teaspoon snipped fresh thyme

In a large saucepan cook the mushrooms, celery, carrot, and onion in hot margarine or butter until crisp-tender. Stir in water, bouillon granules, and pepper.

Bring to boiling; stir in orzo. Return to boiling; reduce heat. Simmer, uncovered, for 5 to 8 minutes or until orzo is tender but still firm. Stir in turkey, parsley, and thyme; heat through. Makes 4 servings.

Herb Tip: When using herbs in cooking, it's best to add dried herbs during the beginning of cooking and fresh later in the process. If fresh are added too early, the flavor will not be as fresh or pronounced. You will note that in most cases the recipes will instruct you when to add dried herbs and when to add fresh herbs when both are options.

Nutrition Facts per serving: 199 cal., 6 g total fat (2 g sat. fat), 40 mg chol., 767 mg sodium, 17 g carbo., 2 g fiber, 19 g pro. ▶ Exchanges: ½ Starch, 1½ Vegetable, 2 Meat

In a large saucepan bring chicken broth to boiling. Add the onion, sweet pepper, carrot, and garlic. Return to boiling; reduce heat. Simmer, uncovered, for 10 minutes.

Meanwhile, cut turkey into thin strips. Lightly coat a medium skillet with nonstick cooking spray. Heat skillet over medium heat. Add turkey strips to the skillet and stir-fry about 3 minutes or until tender and no longer pink. Remove skillet from heat; set aside.

Add pasta, dried thyme (if using), and pepper to broth mixture in saucepan. Return to boiling; reduce heat. Simmer, uncovered, for 5 to 6 minutes or until pasta is tender but still slightly firm. Stir in turkey and spinach. Cook for 1 to 2 minutes more or just until spinach is wilted. Stir in fresh thyme, if using. To serve, ladle soup into bowls. Sprinkle each serving with Parmesan cheese. Makes 8 servings.

3 14½-ounce cans reduced-sodium chicken broth

1 medium onion, chopped

1 small red and/or yellow sweet pepper, chopped

1 medium carrot, sliced

3 cloves garlic, minced

6 ounces turkey breast tenderloins

Nonstick cooking spray

3 ounces dried small pasta, such as tiny bow ties

1 teaspoon snipped fresh thyme or ¼ teaspoon dried thyme, crushed

¼ teaspoon black pepper

3 cups torn fresh spinach leaves

2 tablespoons finely shredded Parmesan cheese

turkey and pasta soup

Small pasta such as tiny shell macaroni or broken linguine let the pasta cook quickly so the vegetables retain their flavor and nutrition.

Nutrition Facts per serving: 320 cal., 13 g total fat (2 g sat. fat), 65 mg chol., 704 mg sodium, 38 g carbo., 5 g fiber, 15 g pro. ▶ Exchanges: 2 Starch, 2 Vegetable, 1 Meat, 1½ Fat

1 tablespoon olive oil

1 large leek, thinly sliced

3 cloves garlic, minced

1 14½-ounce can beef broth

¾ cup water

¼ teaspoon crushed red pepper (optional)

5 cups coarsely chopped broccoli rabe* (6 ounces)

1 14½-ounce can no-salt-added stewed tomatoes

1 9-ounce package refrigerated chicken-filled or cheese-filled ravioli

1 tablespoon snipped fresh rosemary or 1 teaspoon dried rosemary, crushed

¼ cup grated Asiago cheese

Fresh rosemary (optional)

In a large saucepan heat oil over medium heat. Add leek and garlic. Cook for 5 minutes, stirring occasionally. Stir in broth, water, and, if desired, red pepper; bring to boiling.

Stir in broccoli rabe, undrained tomatoes, ravioli, and rosemary. Return to boiling; reduce heat. Simmer, covered, for 7 to 8 minutes or until broccoli rabe and ravioli are tender. Ladle into bowls; top with cheese. If desired, garnish with rosemary. Makes 4 servings.

*Note: If broccoli rabe is not available, substitute 1 small head escarole, a mildly bitter green. Coarsely chop and add to stew during the last 2 minutes of cooking. Or, substitute regular broccoli, cooking it the same amount of time as the broccoli rabe.

In this stew, broccoli rabe stars with plump ravioli. Broccoli rabe is bitter in flavor—substitute regular broccoli if you prefer.

tuscan ravioli stew

Nutrition Facts per serving: 262 cal., 8 g total fat (3 g sat. fat), 16 mg chol., 722 mg sodium, 35 g carbo., 4 g fiber, 14 g pro. ▶ Exchanges: 1 Starch, 1 Vegetable, 1 Meat, ½ Milk, ▶

3 cups sliced fresh shiitake mushrooms or other fresh mushrooms

¾ cup thinly sliced leeks or ½ cup thinly sliced green onions

1 tablespoon margarine or butter

2 cups chicken or vegetable broth

2 cups fat-free milk

2 tablespoons cornstarch

4 ounces thinly sliced smoked salmon (lox-style), flaked

2 tablespoons dry sherry

1 tablespoon snipped fresh dill

In a large saucepan cook the mushrooms and leeks or green onions in hot margarine or butter until tender. Stir in the chicken broth. Bring to boiling.

Meanwhile, in a small bowl combine milk and cornstarch; stir into mushroom mixture. Cook and stir over medium heat until thickened and bubbly. Cook and stir for 2 minutes more. Stir in salmon, sherry, and dill; heat through. Makes 4 servings.

Smoked Salmon Tip: Lox-style salmon is a cold-smoked, brine-cured salmon. Some lox is saltier than other types of smoked salmon unless a little sugar is added to the brine. Lox is popular in American-Jewish cuisine and is often served on bagels with cream cheese.

Although simple, this soup tastes great because it's pumped with highly flavored ingredients—smoked salmon, sherry, and dill.

sherried smoked
salmon soup

spanish-style soup

Pink shrimp, emerald peas, red peppers, and tender pork—all part of classic Spanish paella—make up this rice-based soup.

In a large saucepan cook pork cubes in hot oil for 4 to 5 minutes or until no longer pink; remove pork from pan. In the same pan cook the green onions, sweet pepper, and garlic in drippings for 2 minutes.

Stir in broth, rice, bay leaf, oregano, salt, ground red pepper, and turmeric. Bring to boiling; reduce heat. Simmer, covered, for 15 minutes. Stir in cooked pork, shrimp, and peas.

Simmer, covered, for 3 to 5 minutes more or until shrimp are opaque. Remove the bay leaf. To serve, ladle into serving bowls and, if desired, sprinkle with fresh parsley. Makes 4 servings.

Broth Tip: Eating salty foods or foods high in sodium, such as broth, can cause you to retain water, an unwanted condition for weight watchers. Use low-sodium broth to keep your sodium intake in check. Or if you prefer to use regular broth in this soup, try to keep your sodium intake to a minimum the rest of the day to help curb water retention.

8 ounces lean boneless pork, cut into ¾-inch cubes

1 teaspoon cooking oil

½ cup thinly sliced green onions

⅓ cup chopped red sweet pepper

1 clove garlic, minced

2 14½-ounce cans reduced-sodium chicken broth

½ cup long grain rice

1 bay leaf

½ teaspoon dried oregano, crushed

¼ teaspoon salt

⅛ teaspoon ground red pepper

⅛ teaspoon ground turmeric

8 ounces peeled and deveined fresh shrimp

1 cup frozen peas

1 tablespoon snipped fresh parsley (optional)

Nutrition Facts per serving: 256 cal., 7 g total fat (2 g sat. fat), 113 mg chol., 860 mg sodium, 25 g carbo., 2 g fiber, 23 g pro. ▶ Exchanges: 1½ Starch, 2½ Meat

spiced seafood stew

The seafood trio of shrimp, scallops, and mussels, simmered with aromatic spices, makes a welcome dinner on a cool fall night.

Thaw shrimp and scallops, if frozen. Peel and devein shrimp, leaving tails intact. Rinse shrimp and scallops; pat dry. Scrub mussels; remove beards. In a large bowl combine 2 cups water and 3 tablespoons salt; soak mussels in salt water for 15 minutes. Drain; rinse. Repeat twice.

In a large saucepan cook onion and garlic in hot oil until tender. Stir in cumin, cinnamon, and red pepper; cook and stir for 1 minute. Stir in broth, tomatoes, salt, and saffron. Bring to boiling; add shrimp, scallops, and mussels. Return to boiling; reduce heat. Simmer, covered, about 5 minutes or until mussel shells open. If desired, garnish with flat-leaf parsley. Makes 4 servings.

8 ounces fresh or frozen medium shrimp in shells

8 ounces fresh or frozen scallops

8 ounces (8 to 12) fresh mussels in shells

1 cup finely chopped onion

4 cloves garlic, minced

1 tablespoon olive oil

1 teaspoon ground cumin

½ teaspoon ground cinnamon

¼ teaspoon ground red pepper

1 cup fish or vegetable broth

1 cup finely chopped tomatoes

¼ teaspoon salt

⅛ teaspoon ground saffron

Flat-leaf parsley (optional)

Nutrition Facts per serving: 187 cal., 6 g total fat (1 g sat. fat), 116 mg chol., 503 mg sodium, 12 g carbo., 1 g fiber, 23 g pro. ▶ Exchanges: 1½ Vegetable, 3 Meat

easy cassoulet

You won't believe the results when this traditionally long-cooking dish is transformed into a fast, healthful meal.

Nonstick cooking spray

6 ounces **lean boneless pork, cut into bite-size pieces**

1 large **onion, cut into thin wedges**

2 medium **carrots, thinly sliced**

2 cloves **garlic, minced**

½ cup **reduced-sodium chicken broth**

½ teaspoon **dried thyme, crushed**

1 14½-ounce can **diced tomatoes**

¼ cup **dry white wine or reduced-sodium chicken broth**

2 15-ounce cans **Great Northern beans, drained and rinsed**

6 ounces **fully cooked smoked turkey sausage, cut into bite-size pieces**

1 tablespoon **snipped fresh parsley**

Lightly coat a large saucepan or a 4-quart Dutch oven with nonstick cooking spray; heat over medium heat. Add pork; cook and stir for 2 to 3 minutes or until pork is lightly browned. Add the onion, carrots, garlic, chicken broth, and thyme. Bring to boiling; reduce heat. Simmer, covered, for 6 to 8 minutes or until pork and vegetables are just tender.

Stir in undrained tomatoes, wine or chicken broth, and beans. Mash beans slightly; stir in sausage. Bring mixture just to boiling. Before serving, sprinkle with parsley. Makes 5 servings.

THE BENEFITS OF BELIEVING ▶ MIND·BODY·SPIRIT

Take a few minutes each day to get in touch with your spiritual side. Studies indicate that you're likely to live longer if you attend a religious institution or privately pray as a way of coping. No one is sure why this is so, but praying appears to have strong benefits for your well-being.

Nutrition Facts per serving: 218 cal., 6 g total fat (2 g sat. fat), 37 mg chol., 575 mg sodium, 24 g carbo., 6 g fiber, 18 g pro. ▶ Exchanges: 1 Starch, 1 Vegetable, 2 Meat

Nutrition Facts per serving: 286 cal., 5 g total fat (1 g sat. fat), 60 mg chol., 778 mg sodium, 31 g carbo., 6 g fiber, 27 g pro. ▶ Exchanges: 1 Starch, 1 Vegetable, 3 Meat

2 teaspoons cooking oil

1 small onion, chopped

4 cloves garlic, minced

12 ounces pork tenderloin, cut into ¾-inch cubes

2 teaspoons chili powder

2 teaspoons ground cumin

1 yellow or red sweet pepper, cut into ½-inch pieces

1 cup beer or beef broth

½ cup picante sauce or salsa

1 to 2 tablespoons finely chopped chipotle peppers in adobo sauce

1 16-ounce can red beans or pinto beans, drained and rinsed

½ cup fat-free or light dairy sour cream

¼ cup snipped fresh cilantro

In a large saucepan heat oil over medium-high heat. Add the onion and garlic to saucepan; cook about 3 minutes or until tender. Toss pork with chili powder and cumin; add to saucepan. Cook and stir about 3 minutes or until pork is brown.

Stir sweet pepper, beer or beef broth, picante sauce or salsa, and chipotle peppers into pork mixture in saucepan. Bring to boiling; reduce heat. Simmer, uncovered, about 5 minutes or until pork is just tender. Add beans; heat through. Ladle into bowls; top with sour cream and cilantro. Makes 4 servings.

This quick-to-fix pork stew gets a jump-start from the robust flavors of chipotle peppers, cumin, and picante sauce.

chunky pork chili

Nutrition Facts per serving: 289 cal., 8 g total fat (2 g sat. fat), 65 mg chol., 438 mg sodium, 17 g carbo., 4 g fiber, 28 g pro. ▶ Exchanges: ½ Starch, 2 Vegetable, 3 Meat

1 pound lean, boneless beef round, cut into 1-inch cubes

1 tablespoon olive oil

1 small onion, chopped

1 cup dry white wine

1 teaspoon dried herbes de Provence, crushed

¼ teaspoon salt

¼ teaspoon black pepper

2 cups water

8 small new potatoes (about 6 ounces)

8 pearl onions, peeled

1 large tomato, peeled, cored, seeded, and chopped

¼ cup niçoise olives, pitted, or pitted kalamata olives

2 tablespoons drained capers

8 ounces haricots verts or small green beans, trimmed and cut into 3-inch lengths

1 tablespoon chopped fresh flat-leaf parsley

In a Dutch oven brown half of the meat in hot oil on all sides. Remove meat from pan using a slotted spoon. Add remaining meat and chopped onion to drippings in pan. Cook until meat is brown and onion is tender, about 3 to 5 minutes. Drain off any fat from pan. Return all of meat to pan.

Add wine to the pan, stirring to scrape up the browned bits from bottom of pan. Add herbes de Provence, salt, pepper, and the water. Bring to boiling; reduce heat. Simmer, covered, for 1¼ hours or until meat is nearly tender. Add the potatoes and pearl onions. Return to boiling; reduce heat. Simmer, covered, for 30 minutes or until meat and vegetables are tender. Stir in tomato, olives, and capers; heat through.

Meanwhile, in a medium saucepan cook haricots verts or small green beans, covered, in a small amount of boiling water for 5 to 7 minutes or until tender.

To serve, divide the stew among four bowls. Serve with haricots verts or green beans and garnish with parsley. Makes 4 servings.

Herbes de Provence, niçoise olives, and capers give this dish its country French accent. Long, slow simmering tenderizes the meat.

french beef stew

Nutrition Facts per serving: 251 cal., 3 g total fat (0 g sat. fat), 12 mg chol., 753 mg sodium, 41 g carbo., 9 g fiber, 19 g pro. ▶ Exchanges: 2 Starch, ½ Vegetable, 1½ Meat

2 cups **dry black-eyed peas, rinsed and drained**

2 **14½-ounce cans reduced-sodium chicken broth**

1½ cups **water**

4 medium **carrots, sliced ½ inch thick**

1 cup **reduced-sodium ham cut into ½-inch pieces**

2 stalks **celery, sliced**

½ cup **chopped onion**

1 teaspoon **dried sage, crushed, or 1 tablespoon snipped fresh sage**

1 teaspoon **dried thyme, crushed, or 1 tablespoon snipped fresh thyme**

¼ teaspoon **ground red pepper**

1 tablespoon **lemon juice**

In a 3-quart saucepan bring 4 cups water and black-eyed peas to boiling; reduce heat. Simmer for 2 minutes. Remove from heat. Cover and let stand for 1 hour. (Or, omit simmering; soak beans in the 4 cups water overnight in a covered pan.) Drain and rinse beans.

In a 4-quart crockery cooker combine broth, the 1½ cups water, carrots, ham, celery, onion, dried sage (if using), dried thyme (if using), and red pepper. Stir in drained black-eyed peas.

Cover and cook on low-heat setting for 11 to 12 hours or on high-heat setting for 4½ to 5½ hours. Just before serving, stir in fresh sage (if using), fresh thyme (if using), and lemon juice. Makes 6 servings.

ham and black-eyed pea soup

The aroma of Southern comfort food greets you when you walk in the door at the end of the day, compliments of your crockery cooker.

endive, ham and bean soup

The slightly bitter flavor of endive is matched with ham and beans in this satisfying soup. It's perfect fare for a cold winter night.

In a large saucepan cook onion, carrot, celery, and garlic in hot oil until tender. Stir in the chicken broth, kidney beans, ham, and dried sage, if using.

Bring to boiling. Stir in the curly endive or Chinese cabbage; reduce heat. Simmer, covered, about 3 minutes or just until endive wilts. Stir in the fresh sage, if using. Makes 4 servings.

Soup Tip: Soups are excellent foods to add to your menu plans. Soups fill you up (especially those that contain beans), take longer to eat than some other types of foods, and make great leftovers (keeping you from being tempted to go to Fast Food Freddie's drive through because you have nothing in the house to eat).

1 medium onion, chopped

1 medium carrot, chopped

1 stalk celery, chopped

2 cloves garlic, minced

1 tablespoon olive oil or cooking oil

4 cups reduced-sodium chicken broth

1 19-ounce can white kidney beans, drained and rinsed

⅔ cup chopped reduced-sodium ham

¾ teaspoon dried sage, crushed, or 1 teaspoon snipped fresh sage

3 cups shredded curly endive or Chinese cabbage

Nutrition Facts per serving: 175 cal., 5 g total fat (1 g sat. fat), 11 mg chol., 1,032 mg sodium, 24 g carbo., 8 g fiber, 16 g pro. ▶ Exchanges: 1½ Starch, 2 Vegetable, 2 Meat

spring vegetable soup

Enjoy first-of-the-season garden-fresh vegetables in this splendid spring soup.

Remove tough outer green leaves from artichokes. The inside leaves will be more tender and greenish-yellow. Snip off about 1 inch from the leaf tops, cutting where the green meets the yellow. Trim the stems. Quarter the artichokes lengthwise; set aside.

In a 4-quart Dutch oven combine broth, onions, pancetta or bacon, fennel seed, and pepper. Bring to boiling; reduce heat. Simmer, covered, for 10 minutes. Add artichokes and beans; cook for 5 minutes. Add asparagus and fennel; cook about 5 minutes more or until vegetables are tender.

To serve, ladle into soup bowls. Top with snipped fennel leaves. Makes 8 servings.

*Note: For 2 cups cooked fava beans, purchase 2 pounds fresh fava beans in the pod. To cook fresh or frozen fava beans, simmer, covered, in a small amount of boiling water for 15 to 25 minutes or until tender. Drain and cool slightly. When cool, remove skins from fava beans.

- 12 baby artichokes
- 6 cups chicken broth
- 1 cup small boiling onions, peeled and halved, or pearl onions
- 4 ounces pancetta or 5 slices bacon, crisp-cooked, drained, and cut into small pieces
- 1 teaspoon fennel seed, crushed
- ¼ teaspoon black pepper
- 2 cups cooked* or canned fava beans, rinsed and drained
- 12 ounces asparagus, cut into 1-inch pieces
- 1 medium fennel bulb, trimmed and chopped
- ¼ cup snipped fennel leaves

Nutrition Facts per serving: 152 cal., 3 g total fat (1 g sat. fat), 4 mg chol., 695 mg sodium, 21 g carbo., 6 g fiber, 11 g pro. ▶ Exchanges: 1 Starch, 1 Vegetable, 1 Meat

bean and pasta soup

Thanks to the beans, this ham, pasta, and spinach combination satisfies your hunger and fills you up. Serve with a simple greens salad.

In a Dutch oven bring the beans and 4 cups of the cold water to boiling; reduce heat. Simmer for 2 minutes. Remove from heat. Cover and let stand for 1 hour. (Or, omit simmering; soak beans in 4 cups water overnight in a covered pan.) Drain and rinse beans.

In the same Dutch oven combine drained beans, the remaining 5½ cups water, ham, onion, celery, bouillon granules, garlic, dried basil (if using), and pepper. Cover and simmer about 1½ hours or until beans are tender. Mash beans slightly; bring to boiling. Stir in pasta. Cook, uncovered, for 8 to 10 minutes or just until pasta is tender but still firm. Stir in fresh basil (if using) and spinach. Makes 4 servings.

1 cup **dry Great Northern beans, rinsed**

9½ cups **cold water**

½ cup **diced cooked ham**

½ cup **chopped onion**

½ cup **sliced celery**

1 tablespoon **instant beef bouillon granules**

2 cloves **garlic, minced**

1½ teaspoons **dried basil, crushed, or 1 tablespoon snipped fresh basil**

¼ teaspoon **black pepper**

½ cup **small dried pasta (such as tiny shells, macaroni, or bow ties)**

4 cups **torn fresh spinach**

I THINK, THEREFORE I AM ▶ MIND·BODY·SPIRIT

What you think about yourself impacts how you appear to others. If you think you're not too bright, most people will probably think that, too. If you believe you are confident, more than likely others will see you that way. Even if you don't believe good things about yourself, you can talk yourself into it. Eventually, just as you came to believe the negative thoughts about yourself, you will come to believe the positive things.

Nutrition Facts per serving: 285 cal., 2 g total fat (1 g sat. fat), 10 mg chol., 954 mg sodium, 48 g carbo., 2 g fiber, 20 g pro. ▶ Exchanges: 3 Starch, 1 Vegetable, ½ Meat

Nutrition Facts per serving: 258 cal., 6 g total fat (1 g sat. fat), 11 mg chol., 795 mg sodium, 37 g carbo., 4 g fiber, 12 g pro. ▶ Exchanges: 2½ Starch, ½ Meat

4 medium **red potatoes**

Nonstick cooking spray

1 **large onion, coarsely chopped**

2 teaspoons **snipped fresh rosemary or 1 teaspoon dried rosemary, crushed**

1 **bulb garlic**

1 tablespoon **olive oil**

1 14½-ounce can **chicken broth**

1 tablespoon **all-purpose flour**

¼ teaspoon **black pepper**

½ of a 6-ounce package **Canadian-style bacon, chopped (about ½ cup)**

1 cup **fat-free half-and-half**

Fat-free croutons (optional)

Peel and cube 2 of the potatoes. Cube remaining 2 potatoes, leaving skin intact. Lightly coat a 9×9×2-inch baking pan with nonstick cooking spray. Place peeled potatoes on one side of the baking pan and unpeeled potatoes on the other side of pan. Sprinkle onion and snipped rosemary evenly over all. Set aside.

Peel away the dry outer leaves of skin from bulb of garlic; leave skins of cloves intact. Using a sharp knife, cut off the pointed top of the bulb, leaving bulb intact, but exposing the cloves. Place garlic bulb, cut side up, on top of potatoes. Drizzle olive oil over all. Bake, covered, in a 400° oven about 50 minutes or until garlic cloves feel soft and potatoes are tender; cool slightly.

Squeeze garlic bulb to remove the paste from the cloves. In a food processor bowl combine peeled potato mixture, garlic paste, half of the broth, the flour, and pepper. Cover and process until nearly smooth.

Pour the pureed mixture into a medium saucepan. Stir in the Canadian bacon, unpeeled cooked potato mixture, remaining broth, and the half-and-half. Cook and stir over medium heat until slightly thickened and bubbly. Cook and stir for 1 minute more. To serve, ladle into soup bowls. If desired, top each serving with croutons. Makes 4 servings.

This richly flavored soup, scented with roasted garlic, makes a soul-satisfying supper.

roasted potato and bacon soup

black and white bean soup

Aromatic cumin and anise seeds complement this duo of black beans and cannellini beans.

2 large fresh poblano peppers

3 cloves garlic, unpeeled

Olive oil nonstick cooking spray

1 cup finely chopped onion

2 14½-ounce cans vegetable broth

2 15-ounce cans black beans, drained and rinsed

1 15-ounce can cannellini beans or Great Northern beans, drained and rinsed

1 6-ounce can tomato paste

1 tablespoon balsamic vinegar

1½ teaspoons dried marjoram, crushed

1½ teaspoons cumin seed, toasted and crushed

1½ teaspoons anise seed, crushed

To roast peppers, halve peppers lengthwise and remove stems, membranes, and seeds. Place peppers, cut sides down, on a foil-lined baking sheet. Bake in a 425° oven about 20 minutes or until skins are bubbly and brown. Wrap peppers in the foil; let stand for 15 to 20 minutes or until cool enough to handle. Using a paring knife, pull skin off gently and slowly; finely chop peppers.

In a small skillet cook unpeeled garlic cloves for 6 to 8 minutes, turning frequently or until slightly softened and lightly browned. Cool; peel and mince.

Lightly coat a 3-quart saucepan with nonstick cooking spray. Cook garlic, onion, and roasted peppers over medium heat about 3 minutes or until tender. Stir in ½ cup of the broth, scraping up any brown bits from bottom of saucepan.

Add black beans, cannellini beans, remaining broth, tomato paste, vinegar, marjoram, cumin seed, and anise seed. Bring to boiling; reduce heat. Simmer, covered, for 5 minutes. Makes 4 servings.

Nutrition Facts per serving: 265 cal., 2 g total fat (0 g sat. fat), 0 mg chol., 1,145 mg sodium, 59 g carbo., 17 g fiber, 22 g pro. ▶ Exchanges: 3 Starch, 2 Vegetable

Nutrition Facts per serving: 261 cal., 1 g total fat (0 g sat. fat), 0 mg chol., 581 mg sodium, 59 g carbo., 12 g fiber, 12 g pro. ▶ Exchanges: 3 Starch, 1½ Vegetable

Nonstick spray coating

1 medium onion, chopped

1 medium carrot, sliced

1 small yellow or green sweet pepper, cut into ½-inch pieces (½ cup)

1 15-ounce can Great Northern, white kidney, or pinto beans, drained and rinsed

1 14½-ounce can diced tomatoes (undrained)

½ cup apple juice or apple cider

⅓ cup raisins

2 teaspoons chili powder

¾ teaspoon ground cinnamon

¼ teaspoon salt

Several dashes of bottled hot pepper sauce

2 cups hot cooked couscous

¼ cup finely chopped peanuts (optional)

Lightly coat a medium saucepan with nonstick cooking spray. Cook onion, carrot, and sweet pepper in saucepan, covered, over medium-low heat for 8 to 10 minutes or until the carrots are just tender, stirring occasionally.

Stir in the beans, undrained tomatoes, apple juice or cider, raisins, chili powder, cinnamon, salt, and hot pepper sauce. Bring mixture to boiling; reduce heat. Cook, covered, about 5 minutes, stirring occasionally. Serve with hot couscous. If desired, garnish with peanuts. Makes 4 servings.

No-Fat Cooking Tip: Using nonstick cooking spray instead of oil or butter for cooking vegetables keeps the fat and calories low in your recipes. But if you prefer, try cooking vegetables in a small amount of broth, water, or juice. Nonstick pans make cooking with either the nonstick cooking spray or liquid even easier.

Perfume your kitchen with the exotic aroma of this beguiling chili spiced with cinnamon.

tunisian vegetable chili

Nutrition Facts per serving: 122 cal., 3 g total fat (0 g sat. fat), 0 mg chol., 1,290 mg sodium, 23 g carbo., 3 g fiber, 6 g pro. ▶ Exchanges: 1 Starch, 1½ Vegetable

5 yellow sweet peppers*

1 cup chopped onion

4 cloves garlic, minced

1 teaspoon olive oil

3 14½-ounce cans (5¼ cups) vegetable or chicken broth

1 cup chopped potato

1 tablespoon snipped fresh oregano

1 teaspoon snipped fresh thyme

Dairy sour cream (optional)

Fresh chives (optional)

Fresh thyme leaves (optional)

To roast the peppers, quarter peppers; remove and discard stems, seeds, and membranes. Place peppers, cut sides down, on a cookie sheet lined with foil. Press the peppers to flatten. Bake in a 425° oven for 25 to 30 minutes or until pepper skins are blistered and dark. Immediately wrap in the foil; let stand about 15 minutes to steam so the skins peel easily. Using a paring knife, remove the blistered skin from the peppers, gently and slowly pulling it off in strips. Discard skin. Set roasted peppers aside.

In a large saucepan cook onion and garlic in hot oil for 3 to 4 minutes or until tender. Stir in roasted peppers, broth, and potato. Bring to boiling; reduce heat. Simmer, covered, for 15 minutes. Cool mixture slightly. Stir in oregano and thyme.

Place one-third of the pepper mixture in a food processor bowl or blender container. Cover; process or blend until almost smooth. Repeat with remaining pepper mixture. Return all of soup to saucepan; heat through. To serve, ladle soup into bowls. If desired, top each serving with a spoonful of sour cream; garnish with chives and thyme. Makes 4 servings.

*Note: If desired, omit yellow peppers and roasting step and use one 12-ounce jar roasted red sweet peppers, drained.

The golden yellow color of this enticing soup makes it appealing to the eye, and the flavor is indescribably delicious.

roasted yellow pepper soup

1 tablespoon **butter or margarine**

3 cups **peeled, diced butternut squash (about 1 small squash)**

2 cups **thinly sliced carrots (4 medium carrots)**

¾ cup **thinly sliced leeks or chopped onion**

2 14½-ounce cans **reduced-sodium chicken broth**

¼ teaspoon **ground white pepper**

¼ teaspoon **nutmeg**

¼ cup **regular or fat-free half-and-half or light cream**

Fresh tarragon sprigs (optional)

In a large saucepan over medium heat melt butter or margarine. Add squash, carrots, and leeks or onion to pan. Cook, covered, for 8 minutes, stirring occasionally. Add broth. Bring to a boil; reduce heat. Simmer, covered, for 25 minutes or until vegetables are very tender.

Place one-third of the squash mixture in a food processor bowl or blender container. Cover; process or blend until almost smooth. Repeat with remaining mixture. Return mixture to saucepan. Add white pepper and nutmeg. Bring just to boiling. Add half-and-half or light cream; heat through. Ladle into soup bowls. If desired, garnish with fresh tarragon. Makes 6 servings.

butternutsquash
and carrot soup

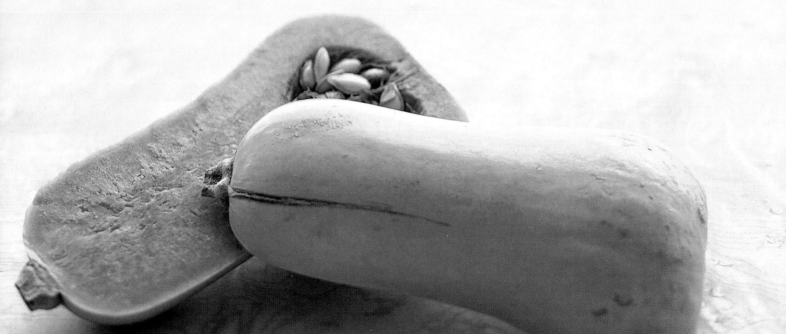

This elegant and smooth squash soup supplies 162 percent of your daily quota for vitamin A.

tomato-basil soup

Pamper yourself with this cooling first-course soup. It requires only four ingredients and a blender to prepare.

Place 3 cups of the tomatoes, the broth, and tomato sauce in a blender container. Cover and blend until smooth.

Stir in the basil and the remaining ½ cup tomatoes. Cover and chill until serving time. If desired, garnish with chives. Makes 4 servings.

Peeling Tomatoes Tip: To peel tomatoes, plunge them into a large saucepan of boiling water for 30 seconds. Immediately rinse them in cold water. Use a paring knife to peel the skins off easily.

5 large tomatoes, peeled, seeded, and coarsely chopped (3½ cups)

1 cup vegetable broth or chicken broth

1 8-ounce can tomato sauce

2 tablespoons snipped fresh basil or 1 teaspoon dried basil, crushed

Snipped fresh chives (optional)

Nutrition Facts per serving: 57 cal., 1 g total fat (0 g sat. fat), 0 mg chol., 604 mg sodium, 13 g carbo., 3 g fiber, 2 g pro. ▶ Exchanges: 2 Vegetable

Nutrition Facts per serving: 223 cal., 6 g total fat (1 g sat. fat), 0 mg chol., 854 mg sodium, 45 g carbo., 9 g fiber, 7 g pro. ▶ Exchanges: 2 Starch, 1 Vegetable, ½ Fruit

½ cup chopped sweet onion (such as Vidalia or Walla Walla)

2 teaspoons grated fresh ginger

1 tablespoon margarine or butter

3 pears, peeled, cored, and sliced

1 15-ounce can pumpkin

1½ cups vegetable broth

1 cup milk

¼ cup light dairy sour cream

½ teaspoon finely shredded lime peel

1 tablespoon lime juice

Lime peel (optional)

In a large saucepan cook onion and ginger in hot margarine or butter until onion is tender. Stir in pears; cook for 1 minute. Stir in pumpkin and vegetable broth. Bring mixture to boiling; reduce heat. Simmer, covered, for 5 minutes more or until pears are tender. Cool slightly.

In a food processor bowl or blender container, cover and process or blend half of the pumpkin mixture at a time about 1 minute or until smooth. Return mixture to saucepan; stir in the milk. Heat through. Season to taste with salt and pepper.

Meanwhile, stir together sour cream, lime peel, and lime juice. Drizzle some of the sour cream mixture over each serving of soup. If desired, garnish with additional lime peel. Makes 6 servings.

When you want a festive soup, try this flavorful creation. Canned pumpkin makes it convenient to make. Serve with herbed muffins.

gingered pumpkin pear soup

creamy strawberry soup

Count on this creamy soup when strawberries are at their best—in the summer. Serve it after a light main-dish salad for a refreshing finish.

In a blender container or food processor bowl place yogurt, milk, strawberries or peaches, and sugar. Cover and blend or process until mixture is smooth.

Cover and chill until serving time. If desired, top with additional fruit and fresh mint. Makes 4 servings.

Gingered Melon Soup: Prepare soup as above except, substitute one 8-ounce container lemon low-fat yogurt for vanilla yogurt and 2 cups cubed honeydew melon for the strawberries. Add 1 teaspoon grated fresh ginger before blending.

1 8-ounce carton **vanilla low-fat yogurt**

1 cup **fat-free milk**

2 cups **ripe strawberries or peaches**

2 teaspoons **sugar**

Sliced fruit (optional)

Fresh mint (optional)

Nutrition Facts per serving: 100 cal., 1 g total fat (1 g sat. fat), 5 mg chol., 72 mg sodium, 18 g carbo., 2 g fiber, 5 g pro. ▶ Exchanges: 1 Fruit, ½ Milk

greens, grair

s, sides

6 ounces dried vermicelli or thin spaghetti

¼ cup reduced-sodium soy sauce

¼ cup chicken broth or vegetable broth

2 tablespoons reduced-fat peanut butter spread

1 tablespoon fresh lime juice

1 teaspoon minced garlic

1 teaspoon minced ginger or ½ teaspoon ground ginger

½ teaspoon crushed red pepper

1½ cups shredded or chopped cooked chicken

1 red sweet pepper, cut into thin bite-size strips

3 green onions, cut diagonally into ½-inch pieces

¼ cup snipped fresh cilantro

Lime wedges

2 tablespoons finely chopped peanuts (optional)

Cook pasta according to package directions. Drain and set aside.

In a saucepan combine soy sauce, broth, peanut butter, lime juice, garlic, ginger, and crushed red pepper. Cook and stir over low heat until peanut butter is melted.

Add cooked pasta; toss to coat. Stir in chicken, sweet pepper, green onions, and cilantro. Serve with lime wedges. If desired, sprinkle each serving with peanuts. Makes 4 servings.

Peanuts, which are high in "good" fats, are a flavorful and healthful substitute for oil in this lively pasta and chicken salad.

thai noodle salad

orange-chicken tabbouleh salad

Ideal for a summer buffet or lunch, this salad requires no more cooking than boiling the water.

In a medium bowl pour boiling water over bulgur. Let stand for 30 minutes. Drain excess liquid.

Meanwhile, finely shred enough peel from oranges to make 2 teaspoons. Section oranges over a bowl to catch juices. Cover and chill orange sections until serving time. Measure and reserve ¼ cup of the orange juice.

In a large bowl stir together drained bulgur, orange peel, reserved orange juice, cucumber, chicken, parsley, green onion, mint, oil, and salt. Cover; chill for 4 to 24 hours, stirring occasionally. Just before serving, fold in orange sections. Serve on romaine-lined plates. Makes 4 servings.

1½ cups **boiling water**

¾ cup **bulgur**

2 **oranges**

2 cups **chopped, seeded cucumber**

1½ cups **chopped cooked chicken**

2 tablespoons **snipped fresh parsley**

2 tablespoons **chopped green onion**

1 tablespoon **snipped fresh mint or 1 teaspoon dried mint, crushed**

1 tablespoon **olive oil or salad oil**

½ teaspoon **salt**

Romaine leaves

Nutrition Facts per serving: 262 cal., 8 g total fat (2 g sat. fat), 51 mg chol., 327 mg sodium, 28 g carbo., 8 g fiber, 21 g pro. ▸ **Exchanges:** 1 Starch, ½ Vegetable, ½ Fruit, 2 Meat

sesame chicken kabob salad

Sweet and sour Asian flavors glaze the tender strips of chicken on these festive kabobs.

4 medium skinless, boneless chicken breast halves (1 pound total)

16 fresh pineapple chunks (1 cup)

1 yellow sweet pepper, cut into 1-inch pieces

3 tablespoons rice vinegar or white wine vinegar

2 tablespoons water

1 tablespoon salad oil

1 tablespoon soy sauce

1 teaspoon toasted sesame oil

½ teaspoon dry mustard

1 tablespoon bottled plum sauce or bottled chili sauce

2 cups chopped red cabbage

2 cups chopped bok choy or iceberg lettuce

16 to 24 snow pea pods, strings and tips removed

½ cup sliced fresh mushrooms

Cut each chicken breast half into 4 lengthwise strips. On each of eight 6-inch skewers, thread 2 each of the chicken strips, pineapple, and sweet pepper.

For dressing, in a screw-top jar combine vinegar, water, salad oil, soy sauce, sesame oil, and dry mustard. Cover and shake well. Reserve 2 tablespoons of the dressing. Cover remaining dressing; chill until needed.

Stir together the 2 tablespoons reserved dressing and plum sauce or chili sauce. Brush over kabobs.

Grill kabobs on the rack of an uncovered grill directly over medium coals for 10 to 12 minutes or until chicken is tender and no longer pink, turning once halfway through grilling.

Combine the red cabbage and bok choy or lettuce; divide greens mixture among 4 serving plates. Top with kabobs, pea pods, and mushrooms. Shake dressing; drizzle over salads. Makes 4 servings.

Nutrition Facts per serving: 229 cal., 8 g total fat (2 g sat. fat), 59 mg chol., 332 mg sodium, 15 g carbo., 3 g fiber, 24 g pro. ▶ Exchanges: 1 Vegetable, ½ Fruit, 3 Meat

The peppercorn-spiked vinaigrette is what makes this salad special.
Fresh strawberries aren't required—use frozen instead.

chicken and fruit salad

8 cups mesclun or 6 cups torn romaine and 2 cups torn curly endive or chicory

2½ cups cooked chicken or turkey, cut into bite-size strips (12 ounces)

2 cups sliced, peeled kiwifruit and/or sliced star fruit

1½ cups fresh enoki mushrooms

1 cup cherry tomatoes, halved

1 recipe Strawberry-Peppercorn Vinaigrette

Divide greens among 4 serving plates. Top each serving with chicken or turkey strips, kiwifruit and/or star fruit, mushrooms, and tomatoes.

Drizzle Strawberry-Peppercorn Vinaigrette over salads. Makes 4 servings.

Strawberry-Peppercorn Vinaigrette: In a blender container or food processor bowl combine 1 cup cut-up fresh or frozen strawberries (thaw frozen strawberries), 2 tablespoons red wine vinegar, and ⅛ teaspoon cracked black pepper. Cover and blend or process until smooth. Makes about 1 cup.

Nutrition Facts per serving: 251 cal., 8 g total fat (2 g sat. fat), 84 mg chol., 102 mg sodium, 15 g carbo., 5 g fiber, 31 g pro. ▶ Exchanges: 2 Vegetable, ½ Fruit, 3½ Meat

Nutrition Facts per serving: 195 cal., 8 g total fat (2 g sat. fat), 131 mg chol., 169 mg sodium, 17 g carbo., 1 g fiber, 16 g pro. ▶ Exchanges: 1½ Vegetable, ½ Fruit, 2 Meat, ½ Fat

1 pomelo or large white grapefruit

1 orange

Fresh orange juice

1 tablespoon salad oil

1 tablespoon honey

1 tablespoon lime juice

1 tablespoon lemon juice

2 cloves garlic, minced

⅛ teaspoon ground white pepper

2 medium fennel bulbs, thinly sliced

1 medium onion, thinly sliced

1 tablespoon cooking oil

24 peeled, deveined medium shrimp (about 1 pound)

Boston or Bibb lettuce leaves

Section pomelo or grapefruit and orange over a small bowl to catch juices; add enough fresh orange juice to equal ¼ cup.

For dressing, add salad oil, honey, lime juice, lemon juice, garlic, and white pepper to reserved juices. Whisk until combined. Set dressing aside.

Cook the fennel and onion in hot cooking oil for 2 minutes; cool to room temperature.

Meanwhile, rinse shrimp; pat dry. Cook in boiling water about 2 minutes or until shrimp turn opaque; drain. Rinse with cold water; drain again.

Arrange lettuce on 4 plates. Place onion and fennel mixture in center; arrange shrimp, pomelo or grapefruit sections, and orange sections around center. Drizzle with dressing. Makes 4 servings.

Pomelo, grapefruit's sweeter cousin, joins orange, lemon, and lime to make a sprightly seafood dressing.

fennel and shrimp salad

greek-style shrimp salad

Transport yourself to the Aegean coast with the robust and healthful Mediterranean flavors of shrimp, feta, lemon, and oregano.

Thaw shrimp, if frozen. Peel and devein shrimp, leaving tails intact. Rinse shrimp; pat dry. In a small bowl combine shrimp and half of the Lemon-Oregano Vinaigrette. Cover and marinate at room temperature for 30 minutes. Cover; chill remaining Lemon-Oregano Vinaigrette.

Meanwhile, in a large bowl combine greens, cucumber, tomato, onion, and radishes; toss to combine. Set aside.

Drain shrimp, reserving marinade. Thread shrimp onto eight 8-inch metal skewers, leaving ¼ inch between pieces. Grill on the greased rack of an uncovered grill directly over medium coals for 6 to 8 minutes or until shrimp are opaque, turning and brushing once with reserved marinade. Discard any remaining marinade. To serve, divide greens mixture among 4 serving plates. Sprinkle with feta cheese. Top each salad with 2 skewers of grilled shrimp. Serve with remaining Lemon-Oregano Vinaigrette. Makes 4 servings.

Lemon-Oregano Vinaigrette: In a small bowl stir together 2 tablespoons powdered fruit pectin; 2 teaspoons snipped fresh oregano or ½ teaspoon dried oregano, crushed; 1 teaspoon sugar; ⅛ teaspoon pepper; and dash salt. Stir in ⅓ cup water; 3 tablespoons lemon juice; 3 tablespoons white wine vinegar; 1 teaspoon Dijon-style mustard; and 1 small clove garlic, minced. Cover and refrigerate for up to 3 days. Makes about ⅔ cup.

1 pound fresh or frozen large shrimp in shells

1 recipe Lemon-Oregano Vinaigrette

4 cups torn mixed salad greens

1 medium cucumber, quartered lengthwise and cut into ¼-inch slices

1 medium tomato, cut into thin wedges

¼ cup chopped red onion

¼ cup thinly sliced radishes

¼ cup crumbled feta cheese (1 ounce)

Nutrition Facts per serving: 138 cal., 3 g total fat (1 g sat. fat), 136 mg chol., 331 mg sodium, 13 g carbo., 2 g fiber, 17 g pro. ▶ Exchanges: 2½ Vegetable, 1½ Meat

Nutrition Facts per serving: 311 cal., 11 g total fat (3 g sat. fat), 51 mg chol., 998 mg sodium, 32 g carbo., 4 g fiber, 20 g pro. ▶ Exchanges: 1 Starch, 2 Vegetable, ½ Fruit, 2 Meat, 1 Fa

1½ pounds **pork tenderloin,** cut into ½-inch slices

⅓ cup **water**

¼ cup **dry sherry**

¼ cup **soy sauce**

4 teaspoons **grated fresh ginger**

3 cloves **garlic, minced**

¼ cup **hoisin sauce**

2 tablespoons **brown sugar**

2 tablespoons **rice vinegar or white wine vinegar**

1 tablespoon **salad oil**

1 teaspoon **toasted sesame oil**

8 cups **torn fresh spinach**

4 cups **torn Boston lettuce**

6 thin **red onion slices, separated into rings**

1 tablespoon **sesame seed, toasted**

3 cups **sliced, pitted plums**

Place meat in a plastic bag set in a shallow dish. For marinade, combine the water, sherry, soy sauce, ginger, and garlic. Reserve 2 tablespoons for dressing. Pour remaining marinade over meat; seal bag. Marinate in the refrigerator for 1 hour.

Drain meat, discarding marinade. Grill meat on the rack of an uncovered grill directly over medium coals for 10 to 12 minutes or until a meat thermometer registers 160°, turning once halfway through grilling.

For dressing, in a saucepan stir together reserved marinade, hoisin sauce, brown sugar, vinegar, and salad oil; bring to boiling. Stir in the sesame oil. Remove the saucepan from heat.

Thinly slice meat into bite-size strips. In a large salad bowl combine meat, spinach, lettuce, onion rings, and sesame seed. Pour hot dressing over salad mixture; toss gently to coat. Divide salad mixture among 6 plates. Arrange plum slices around each salad. Makes 6 servings.

This salad's flavors are inspired by the cuisine of the Pacific Ocean's Asian nations.

pacific rim grilled pork salad

beef salad with basil dressing

Buttermilk's tangy taste and creamy consistency belie its low-calorie profile, making it the ideal choice for a beef and vegetable salad.

For dressing, stir together buttermilk, mayonnaise dressing or salad dressing, basil, lemon juice, sugar, and pepper. Cover and chill until serving time.

For salad, divide greens among 4 plates. Arrange beef strips, carrots, zucchini, broccoli, and beets on greens. Drizzle chilled dressing over salads. Makes 4 servings.

Dressing Storage Tip: For longer storage of dressing, use dried basil instead of fresh basil. Place dressing in an airtight container and refrigerate for up to 1 week.

½ cup **buttermilk**

3 tablespoons **fat-free mayonnaise dressing or salad dressing**

1 tablespoon **snipped fresh basil or 1 teaspoon dried basil, crushed**

1 tablespoon **lemon juice**

1 teaspoon **sugar**

Dash **black pepper**

6 cups **torn mixed salad greens**

8 ounces **lean cooked beef, cut into thin strips**

2 medium **carrots, thinly sliced**

1 small **zucchini, halved lengthwise and sliced**

1 cup **broccoli flowerets**

½ of a 16-ounce can **beets, well drained and cut into thin strips**

MIND·BODY·SPIRIT ▶ VOLUNTEER FOR LONGEVITY

Volunteer and you'll add quality to your life as well as to those you help. Just one hour a week may give more meaning to your life, which in turn may have protective effects on your health. The benefits are especially strong if you don't socialize regularly. Look to hospitals or long-term-care facilities for opportunities.

Nutrition Facts per serving: 175 cal., 5 g total fat (2 g sat. fat), 40 mg chol., 380 mg sodium, 17 g carbo., 5 g fiber, 18 g pro. ▶ Exchanges: 2½ Vegetable, 2 Meat

Nutrition Facts per serving: 242 cal., 12 g total fat (4 g sat. fat), 57 mg chol., 235 mg sodium, 13 g carbo., 3 g fiber, 22 g pro. ▶ Exchanges: 2½ Vegetable, 2½ Meat, 1 Fat

¼ cup lime juice

¼ cup reduced-sodium chicken broth

1 tablespoon snipped fresh cilantro

2 cloves garlic, minced

1½ teaspoons cornstarch

12 ounces boneless beef top sirloin steak, cut into thin bite-size strips

½ teaspoon ground cumin

¼ teaspoon salt

¼ teaspoon black pepper

Nonstick cooking spray

2 small onions, cut into thin wedges

1 medium green, red, and/or yellow sweet pepper, cut into thin strips

1 tablespoon cooking oil

1 10-ounce package torn mixed salad greens (8 cups)

12 cherry tomatoes and/or yellow pear tomatoes, quartered

1 recipe Baked Tortilla Wedges (optional)

Salsa (optional)

In a small bowl combine lime juice, chicken broth, cilantro, garlic, and cornstarch; set aside.

In a small bowl sprinkle beef with cumin, salt, and pepper; toss to coat. Lightly coat a cold wok or large skillet with nonstick cooking spray. Preheat over medium heat. Stir-fry onion and sweet pepper for 3 to 4 minutes or until crisp-tender. Remove vegetables from wok.

Carefully add oil to wok. Add beef strips; stir-fry about 3 minutes or to desired doneness. Push to the sides of the skillet. Stir lime juice mixture; add to skillet. Cook and stir until thickened and bubbly. Cook and stir for 1 minute more. Stir meat and vegetables into sauce mixture; heat through.

To serve, arrange salad greens and tomatoes on 4 serving plates. Divide beef-vegetable mixture among plates. If desired, top with Baked Tortilla Wedges and serve with salsa. Makes 4 servings.

Baked Tortilla Wedges: Cut 2 flour or corn tortillas into 8 wedges. Place wedges on a baking sheet. Lightly coat with nonstick cooking spray. Bake in a 400° oven for 5 minutes. Turn and bake for 3 to 5 minutes more.

Beef strips and sweet peppers—cooked in savory Southwest flavors of lime and cumin—turn a simple salad into a lively meal.

warm fajita salad

herbed black bean salad

This salad is what summer is all about—enjoying the pleasure of homegrown tomatoes and fresh herbs.

1 15-ounce can garbanzo beans, drained and rinsed

1 15-ounce can black beans, drained and rinsed

3 medium tomatoes, seeded and chopped (1½ cups)

¼ cup snipped fresh basil

¼ cup snipped fresh oregano

2 green onions, sliced (¼ cup)

1 clove garlic, minced

½ teaspoon salt

¼ teaspoon black pepper

Fresh oregano (optional)

In a medium bowl combine the garbanzo beans, black beans, tomatoes, basil, oregano, green onions, garlic, salt, and pepper.

Let salad stand at room temperature for 30 minutes to 2 hours to allow the flavors to blend. If desired, garnish with additional oregano. Makes 4 servings.

Bean Tips: Because beans are so high in protein, they are excellent substitutes for meat. Beans are also great sources of fiber, phosphorus, iron, and calcium.

Substitute cooked beans for canned beans if you like. Approximately 1¾ cups cooked beans equals one 15-ounce can of beans.

Nutrition Facts per serving: 173 cal., 2 g total fat (0 g sat. fat), 0 mg chol., 942 mg sodium, 33 g carbo., 10 g fiber, 12 g pro. ▶ Exchanges: 2 Starch, ½ Vegetable, ½ Meat

Nutrition Facts per serving: 110 cal., 4 g total fat (0 g sat. fat), 0 mg chol., 375 mg sodium, 18 g carbo., 6 g fiber, 7 g pro. ▶ Exchanges: 1 Starch, 1 Vegetable

For dressing, in a small bowl whisk together vinegar, oil, broth or water, mustard, garlic, salt, sugar, and pepper. (Dressing may be prepared, covered, and refrigerated for up to five days before serving.)

In a large bowl combine the greens, beans, and roasted sweet peppers. Add dressing; toss well to coat. Transfer salad to 4 chilled serving plates. If desired, top each serving with croutons and olives. Makes 4 servings.

bitter greens and bean salad

Mellow balsamic vinegar blends with Dijon, forming a dressing with a pleasant contrast of flavors to the bitter greens.

1½ tablespoons **balsamic or white balsamic vinegar**

1 tablespoon **olive oil**

1 tablespoon **reduced-sodium chicken broth or water**

2 teaspoons **Dijon-style mustard**

1 large clove **garlic, minced**

¼ teaspoon **salt**

¼ teaspoon **sugar**

¼ teaspoon **freshly ground black pepper**

6 cups packed **mixed bitter greens (such as Swiss chard, radicchio, or mustard, beet, or collard greens) and/or mesclun**

1 15-ounce can **white kidney beans, drained and rinsed**

½ of a 7-ounce jar **roasted red sweet peppers, rinsed and drained**

¼ cup **garlic croutons (optional)**

8 **niçoise olives (optional)**

Nutrition Facts per serving: 129 cal., 3 g total fat (0 g sat. fat), 0 mg chol., 74 mg sodium, 24 g carbo., 3 g fiber, 5 g pro. ▶ Exchanges: 1½ Starch

1 10-ounce package frozen lima beans

1 10-ounce package frozen whole kernel corn

2 small tomatoes, seeded and chopped

1 tablespoon fresh parsley

¼ cup sliced green onions

¼ cup red wine vinegar

2 tablespoons Italian dressing

¼ teaspoon dry mustard

Kale leaves (optional)

Cook the lima beans and corn according to package directions; drain. In a large bowl combine the lima beans, corn, tomatoes, parsley, and green onions.

In a small bowl whisk together red wine vinegar, Italian dressing, and mustard. Pour over lima bean mixture; toss to coat. Serve at room temperature or chilled. If desired, garnish with kale leaves. Makes 6 to 8 servings.

Lima Bean Tips: If you'd like to substitute fresh lima beans in this recipe, they are available fresh from June until September. Sold in the pods, limas should be placed in a plastic bag after purchasing and refrigerated for up to 1 week. Shell limas just prior to using. To cook fresh lima beans, simmer, covered, in a small amount of boiling water for 15 to 25 minutes or until tender; drain.

This satisfying dish of limas, corn, and tomatoes is perfect when you want a change from the usual marinated bean salad.

autumn succotash salad

lightened waldorf salad

Lemon yogurt and honey flavor this version of a favorite classic fruit salad.

2 cups **cubed fresh pineapple** or one 15¼-ounce can pineapple chunks (juice pack), drained

2 medium **apples and/or pears, cored and coarsely chopped**

½ cup **thinly sliced celery**

½ cup **halved seedless red grapes**

2 **kiwifruits, peeled, halved lengthwise, and sliced**

⅓ cup **fat-free mayonnaise dressing or salad dressing**

⅓ cup **lemon fat-free or low-fat yogurt**

1 tablespoon **honey**

2 tablespoons **walnut pieces, toasted**

Flowering kale or lettuce leaves (optional)

In a large bowl toss together pineapple, apples or pears, celery, grapes, and kiwifruits. In a small bowl stir together the mayonnaise dressing or salad dressing, yogurt, and honey; fold gently into pineapple mixture.

Cover and chill for up to 6 hours. Just before serving, stir in toasted walnuts. If desired, serve on flowering kale or lettuce leaves. Makes 6 to 8 servings.

Pineapple Storage Tip: Refrigerate ripe, fresh pineapple for up to 2 days. Do not store at room temperature. Cut pineapple will last a couple more days if placed in an airtight container in the refrigerator.

Nutrition Facts per serving: 123 cal., 2 g total fat (0 g sat. fat), 0 mg chol., 189 mg sodium, 26 g carbo., 2 g fiber, 2 g pro. ▶ Exchanges: 1½ Fruit, ½ Fat

Nutrition Facts per serving: 122 cal., 1 g total fat (0 g sat. fat), 0 mg chol., 322 mg sodium, 23 g carbo., 5 g fiber, 6 g pro. ▶ Exchanges: 1 Starch, 1½ Vegetable

In a large saucepan bring water and salt to boiling. Add potatoes and cook, covered, for 8 minutes. Add asparagus and sliced fennel; cook for 4 to 6 minutes more or until potatoes are just tender and asparagus and fennel are crisp-tender. Drain well. Arrange vegetables in a shallow serving dish. Cover and chill.

For dressing, in a small bowl stir together mayonnaise dressing or salad dressing, yogurt, green onions, vinegar, fennel leaves, and pepper. Cover and chill. Just before serving, spoon dressing over vegetables. Toss vegetables to coat with dressing. If desired, garnish with fresh fennel leaves. Makes 4 to 6 servings.

1 cup water

¼ teaspoon salt

¾ pound whole tiny new potatoes, quartered (about 9)

12 ounces asparagus, trimmed and cut into 1-inch pieces (1½ cups)

1 medium fennel bulb, thinly sliced (1 cup)

¼ cup fat-free mayonnaise dressing or salad dressing

¼ cup plain fat-free yogurt

2 green onions, thinly sliced (¼ cup)

1 tablespoon white wine vinegar

2 teaspoons snipped fresh fennel leaves

⅛ teaspoon coarsely ground black pepper

Fennel leaves (optional)

potato-fennel salad

Fresh dill, tender asparagus, and bright-orange carrots take the "ho-hum" out of potato salad.

191

fruit salad with cranberry dressing

The brilliant ruby red cranberries brighten this refreshing winter fruit salad. It will become a favorite addition to your holiday menus.

For dressing, in a medium saucepan combine the cranberries and water. Bring to boiling; reduce heat. Simmer, covered, for 4 to 5 minutes or until cranberries just begin to pop. Remove saucepan from heat; stir in sugar and orange juice. When cool, press mixture through a sieve. Discard cranberry skins. Cover and refrigerate the dressing until thoroughly chilled. (The dressing will thicken slightly as it chills.)

To serve, line 6 salad plates with lettuce leaves. Arrange fruit on leaves. Drizzle with dressing. Garnish with mint, if desired. Makes 6 servings.

*Note: To prevent pears from darkening, brush cut edges with lemon juice.

2 cups cranberries

⅓ cup water

1 cup sugar

¼ cup orange juice

2 large seedless oranges, peeled, sliced, and halved

½ large pineapple, peeled, cored, sliced, and cut into wedges

2 large ripe pears, cored and sliced into wedges*

1 kiwifruit, peeled and sliced

Lettuce leaves

Fresh mint leaves (optional)

Nutrition Facts per serving: 231 cal., 1 g total fat (0 g sat. fat), 0 mg chol., 2 mg sodium, 59 g carbo., 5 g fiber, 1 g pro. ▶ Exchanges: 3½ Fruit

sweet-and-sour onions

When you use white and red onions in this simple side dish, it will be as pretty as it is tasty.

In a medium saucepan bring ½ cup water to boiling; add unpeeled pearl onions. Return to boiling; reduce heat. Cook, covered, about 10 minutes or until just tender. Drain onions. Cool slightly; trim ends and remove skins. (Or, cook frozen onions in a medium saucepan according to package directions; drain.)

In the same saucepan melt the margarine or butter over medium heat; stir in vinegar, brown sugar, and pepper. Cook and stir about 30 seconds or until combined. Add the onions and prosciutto or ham to saucepan. Cook, uncovered, over medium heat for 7 to 8 minutes more or until onions are golden brown and slightly glazed, stirring occasionally. Makes 4 servings.

3 cups **pearl white and/or red onions, or one 16-ounce package frozen small whole onions**

2 teaspoons **margarine or butter**

¼ cup **white wine vinegar or balsamic vinegar**

2 tablespoons **brown sugar**

⅛ teaspoon **black pepper**

1 ounce **prosciutto or thinly sliced cooked ham, cut into short, thin strips**

Nutrition Facts per serving: 94 cal., 2 g total fat (0 g sat. fat), 3 mg chol., 372 mg sodium, 16 g carbo., 2 g fiber, 3 g pro. ▶ Exchanges: ½ Starch, 2 Vegetable, ½ Fat

Nutrition Facts per serving: 84 cal., 3 g total fat (0 g sat. fat), 3 mg chol., 241 mg sodium, 11 g carbo., 4 g fiber, 5 g pro. ▶ Exchanges: 1 Starch, ½ Fat

1 ounce thinly sliced prosciutto or cooked ham

¼ cup chopped onion

1 teaspoon olive oil or cooking oil

1 10-ounce package frozen peas

¼ cup water

½ teaspoon instant chicken bouillon granules

¼ teaspoon dried oregano, crushed, or ¾ teaspoon snipped fresh oregano

Dash black pepper

2 tablespoons pine nuts or chopped pecans, toasted

Cut prosciutto or ham into thin strips.

In a medium saucepan cook onion in hot oil until tender. Stir in peas, water, bouillon granules, dried oregano (if using), and pepper. Simmer, covered, for 4 to 5 minutes or until peas are just tender. Stir in prosciutto or ham; heat through. Stir in the fresh oregano (if using) and toasted pine nuts or pecans. Makes 4 servings.

Prosciutto Tip: Prosciutto describes an Italian ham that is unsmoked, seasoned, salt-cured, and then air-dried. Italian prosciuttos are labeled either cotto, which is cooked, or crudo, which is raw but ready-to-eat because it is cured. Prosciutto should be added to pasta or vegetables at the last minute, as overcooking may cause the meat to toughen.

Humble peas become regal with the addition of pine nuts, Italian prosciutto, and oregano.

prosciutto and peas

Nutrition Facts per serving: 192 cal., 4 g total fat (1 g sat. fat), 0 mg chol., 192 mg sodium, 34 g carbo., 8 g fiber, 5 g pro. ▶ Exchanges: 1 Vegetable, 2 Starch

1 green sweet pepper, stemmed, seeded, and quartered

1 yellow sweet pepper, stemmed, seeded, and quartered

1 red onion, cut into ¼-inch slices

6 roma tomatoes, cut in half

1 medium eggplant (about 1 pound), cut into 1-inch slices

1 tablespoon olive oil

1½ cups water

2 tablespoons snipped fresh basil and/or oregano

2 teaspoons olive oil

½ teaspoon salt

1 cup couscous, uncooked

Lightly brush green and yellow peppers, onion, tomatoes, and eggplant with the 1 tablespoon olive oil. Place peppers, onion, and eggplant on the greased grill rack of an uncovered grill directly over medium coals. Place tomatoes in 2 foil pie plates. Place pie plates on grill rack directly over coals.

Grill onion slices, uncovered, for 10 to 15 minutes; sweet peppers for 8 to 10 minutes; and eggplant for about 8 minutes or until vegetables are tender, turning occasionally. Grill tomatoes for 10 to 15 minutes or until heated through, turning once. Remove vegetables from the grill. Cut vegetables into bite-size pieces.

Meanwhile, bring the water to boiling in a medium saucepan. Add basil and/or oregano, the 2 teaspoons olive oil, and salt. Stir in couscous. Remove the saucepan from heat. Cover; let stand for 5 minutes or until liquid is absorbed. To serve, fluff couscous with a fork. Spoon couscous onto a serving platter; top with the grilled vegetables. Makes 6 to 8 servings.

Grilling makes vegetables so sweet and flavorful they don't need a dressing. Herbed couscous makes a delicious companion.

grilled vegetables over couscous

vegetable fried rice

It is necessary to use chilled rice when making this fried rice.
Make the rice ahead and chill it overnight.

In a medium saucepan combine the water and rice. Bring to boiling. Simmer, covered, about 15 minutes. Chill, covered, until needed.

In a 12-inch nonstick skillet heat oil over medium heat. Stir-fry garlic and ginger for 1 minute. Add desired vegetables and bok choy; stir-fry for 3 to 4 minutes or until vegetables are crisp-tender.

Add the chilled rice and soy sauce; stir-fry for 3 minutes. Sprinkle with cilantro or green onions. Makes 8 servings.

2 cups water

1 cup long grain rice

1 tablespoon toasted sesame oil

2 teaspoons minced garlic

2 teaspoons minced ginger

3 cups assorted cut-up fresh vegetables such as sweet peppers, red onion, sliced fresh mushrooms, broccoli flowerets, or matchstick carrots

1½ cups coarsely chopped bok choy

¼ cup reduced-sodium soy sauce

¼ cup snipped fresh cilantro or thinly sliced green onions

THE WRITE WAY TO HEALTH ▶ MIND·BODY·SPIRIT

Putting your pain into words may help ease it. In a 1999 study, 107 people with poor health wrote for 20 minutes for three consecutive days about either a traumatic experience or their plans for the day. Four months later the illnesses of nearly half of those who wrote about a stressful episode improved significantly, compared with one-fourth of those who wrote about mundane things. So, if you're feeling sad, write it down. It might improve your health.

Nutrition Facts per serving: 113 cal., 2 g total fat (0 g sat. fat), 0 mg chol., 269 mg sodium, 21 g carbo., 1 g fiber, 3 g pro. ▶ Exchanges: 1 Starch, ½ Vegetable, ½ Fat

Nutrition Facts per serving: 109 cal., 3 g total fat (1 g sat. fat), 0 mg chol., 130 mg sodium, 21 g carbo., 1 g fiber, 4 g pro. ▶ Exchanges: 1 Starch, ½ Vegetable, ½ Fat

1 cup **chopped onion**

½ cup **chopped red sweet pepper**

½ cup **chopped green sweet pepper**

¼ cup **chorizo sausage, crumbled**

3 to 4 cloves **garlic, minced**

2 teaspoons **olive oil**

2 cups **reduced-sodium chicken broth**

1¼ cups **long grain rice**

In a large ovenproof skillet cook onion, sweet peppers, chorizo, and garlic in hot oil until meat is brown and vegetables are tender. Stir in the chicken broth and rice. Bring to boiling. Remove skillet from heat.

Bake, covered, in a 400° oven about 20 minutes or until the rice is tender and liquid is absorbed. Makes 10 servings.

To cook on the range top: Prepare as above, except do not bake. Simmer, covered, on range top about 20 minutes or until the rice is tender and the liquid is absorbed.

A small amount of chorizo, the spicy Mexican sausage, supplies a punch of flavor. Substitute spicy Italian sausage if you can't find chorizo.

baked chorizo rice

Nutrition Facts per serving: 156 cal., 3 g total fat (0 g sat. fat), 0 mg chol., 381 mg sodium, 28 g carbo., 1 g fiber, 3 g pro. ▶ Exchanges: 1½ Starch, ½ Fat

2 cloves garlic, minced

2 teaspoons olive oil

2½ cups water

1 cup basmati rice

2 teaspoons instant chicken bouillon granules

1½ cups sliced fresh cremini or white mushrooms

4 green onions, thinly sliced (½ cup)

¼ cup chopped red sweet pepper

2 teaspoons finely shredded lemon peel

¼ teaspoon salt

⅛ teaspoon freshly ground black pepper

2 tablespoons chopped pecans, toasted

In a medium saucepan cook garlic in hot oil for 30 seconds. Stir in water, rice, and bouillon granules. Bring to boiling; reduce heat. Simmer, covered, for 10 minutes.

Stir in mushrooms, green onions, sweet pepper, lemon peel, salt, and pepper. Cover and cook for 10 to 15 minutes more or until liquid is absorbed and rice is tender. Stir in pecans. If desired, garnish with lemon slices. Makes 6 servings.

Toasted Nuts Tip: "Toast" nuts quickly and easily in the microwave oven. Place nuts in a 2-cup measure. Cook, uncovered, on 100 percent power (high) until light golden, stirring after 1 minute, then stirring every 30 seconds. Allow 2 to 3 minutes for ½ cup almonds or pecans, 2 to 3 minutes for 1 cup almonds, 3 to 4 minutes for 1 cup pecans, 3 to 4 minutes for ½ cup walnuts, and 3½ to 5 minutes for 1 cup walnuts. Allow to cool on paper towels. Nuts will continue to toast as they stand. Store covered.

Toasty pecans and lemon peel intensify the flavor of slightly sweet, slightly nutty basmati rice in this taste-tempting pilaf.

citrus basmati with pecans

Nutrition Facts per serving: 159 cal., 4 g total fat (0 g sat. fat), 0 mg chol., 296 mg sodium, 28 g carbo., 3 g fiber, 4 g pro. ▶ Exchanges: 1½ Starch, ½ Fat

1½ pounds whole, tiny new potatoes (about 18)

2 tablespoons lemon juice

1 tablespoon olive oil

1 bay leaf

1 teaspoon finely shredded lemon peel

½ teaspoon salt

½ teaspoon dried oregano, crushed

¼ teaspoon freshly ground black pepper

2 cloves garlic, minced

1 tablespoon snipped fresh dill or 1 teaspoon dried dillweed

Scrub potatoes thoroughly with a stiff brush. Cut potatoes into quarters. Place potatoes in a greased 9×9×2-inch baking pan. Combine lemon juice, oil, bay leaf, lemon peel, salt, oregano, pepper, and garlic. Drizzle over potatoes; toss to coat.

Bake, covered, in a 325° oven for 45 minutes. Stir potatoes. Bake, uncovered, for 10 to 20 minutes more or until potatoes are tender and brown on edges. Remove bay leaf. Stir dill into potatoes. Makes 4 servings.

garlic and lemon potatoes

Two lemons should yield the right amount of lemon juice and peel. Use a zester or the smallest holes of a grater for the peel.

creamy potatoes
and mushrooms

This baked potato casserole is a welcome treat for potato lovers.
The earthy flavor of the mushrooms lends it a satisfying richness.

In a small bowl place the dried mushrooms in enough warm water to cover. Let mushrooms soak for 30 minutes. Drain and coarsely chop.

For sauce, in a medium saucepan cook mushrooms and onion in hot oil until the onion is tender. Stir in the flour, salt, and pepper. Add milk all at once. Cook and stir until thickened and bubbly. Remove saucepan from heat. Stir half of the cheese into the sauce. Place half of the sliced potatoes into a greased 1-quart casserole. Cover with half of the sauce. Repeat layering. Sprinkle with the remaining cheese.

Bake, covered, in a 350° oven for 35 minutes. Uncover; bake for 35 minutes more or until potatoes are tender and top is golden brown. Let stand for 5 minutes before serving. Makes 6 servings.

½ cup dried porcini or morel mushrooms (about ⅜ ounce)

1 small onion, thinly sliced

1 tablespoon olive oil

2 tablespoons all-purpose flour

¼ teaspoon salt

⅛ teaspoon black pepper

1¼ cup fat-free milk

½ cup freshly shredded pecorino cheese or Parmesan cheese (2 ounces)

3 medium baking potatoes, peeled and thinly sliced (3 cups)

Nutrition Facts per serving: 167 cal., 5 g total fat (2 g sat. fat), 8 mg chol., 297 mg sodium, 22 g carbo., 2 g fiber, 8 g pro. ▶ Exchanges: 1½ Starch, 1 Fat

Nutrition Facts per serving: 162 cal., 5 g total fat (1 g sat. fat), 0 mg chol., 166 mg sodium, 28 g carbo., 2 g fiber, 2 g pro. ▶ Exchanges: 1½ Starch, 1 Fat

Nonstick cooking spray

1¼ to 1½ pounds **Yukon gold potatoes (3 large or 4 medium)**

4 teaspoons **olive oil**

½ teaspoon **seasoned salt**

⅛ teaspoon **ground red pepper**

Lightly coat a 15×10×1-inch baking pan with nonstick cooking spray; set pan aside.

Peel potatoes; rinse with cold water. Cut potatoes lengthwise into ¼-inch slices. Stack 2 or 3 slices; cut lengthwise into ⅛-inch-wide strips. Repeat with remaining slices. In a large bowl combine potato strips and oil; toss to coat. Arrange in a single layer in prepared pan.

Bake, uncovered, in a 450° oven for 15 minutes. Use a large spatula to turn potato strips. Bake for 12 to 15 minutes more or until crisp and golden brown. Sprinkle potatoes with seasoned salt and ground red pepper; toss to coat. Serve immediately. Makes 4 servings.

Crisp and spicy on the outside, tender and smooth on the inside, these French-style potatoes roast to perfection.

spicy pommes frites

glazed carrots and parsnips

White balsamic vinegar has a mellow, sweet flavor similar to regular balsamic but won't darken the vegetables.

In a medium saucepan cook carrots and parsnips, covered, in a small amount of boiling salted water for 7 to 9 minutes or until crisp-tender. Drain. Add margarine or butter, stirring gently until melted.

For glaze, in a small bowl stir together vinegar, honey, and nutmeg. Pour glaze over vegetables in saucepan, tossing gently to coat. Cook and stir about 1 minute or until heated through. Makes 8 servings.

Parsnip Tip: Parsnips, winter root vegetables shaped like a large carrot, have a sweet, nutty flavor. Look for them in the supermarket January through March. They should be firm with fairly smooth skin and few rootlets. Avoid any that are limp, shriveled, or cracked.

6 medium carrots (about 1 pound), cut into ¼-inch slices

3 medium parsnips (about 1 pound), cut into ¼-inch slices

1 tablespoon margarine or butter

3 tablespoons white balsamic vinegar or white wine vinegar

2 tablespoons honey

¼ teaspoon ground nutmeg

Nutrition Facts per serving: 90 cal., 2 g total fat (0 g sat. fat), 0 mg chol., 56 mg sodium, 19 g carbo., 4 g fiber, 1 g pro. ▶ Exchanges: 3 Vegetable, ½ Fat

lemon-marinated baby vegetables

Be careful not to overcook delicate baby vegetables—they will lose their lovely colors and fresh flavors.

2 tablespoons water

1 tablespoon olive oil

½ teaspoon finely shredded lemon peel

2 tablespoons fresh lemon juice

1 teaspoon Dijon-style mustard

2 teaspoons snipped fresh basil or oregano

1 clove garlic, minced

2 pounds tiny, whole vegetables such as carrots, zucchini, and/or pattypan squash

½ pound sugar snap peas and/or yellow beans

12 cherry tomatoes

Fresh oregano (optional)

For dressing, in a screw-top jar combine water, oil, lemon peel, lemon juice, mustard, basil or oregano, and garlic.

In a large saucepan cook carrots, zucchini, and/or yellow squash in a small amount of water, covered, for 3 minutes. Add sugar snap peas; cook for 2 to 3 minutes more or until vegetables are crisp-tender. Drain; rinse vegetables with cold water. Drain again.

In a large bowl combine the cooked vegetables, tomatoes, and salad dressing, tossing gently to coat. Cover and chill for at least 2 hours or overnight before serving. If desired, garnish with oregano. Makes 8 servings.

Nutrition Facts per serving: 59 cal., 2 g total fat (0 g sat. fat), 0 mg chol., 43 mg sodium, 9 g carbo., 3 g fiber, 2 g pro. ▶ Exchanges: 1½ Vegetable, ½ Fat

asparagus with warm vinaigrette

The lively combination of ginger and apricot nectar creates a noteworthy vinaigrette for fresh asparagus.

Snap off and discard the woody bases of asparagus. If desired, use a vegetable peeler to scrape off scales. Cook, covered, in a small amount of boiling water for 8 to 10 minutes or until asparagus is crisp-tender. Drain.

Meanwhile, for vinaigrette, in a small saucepan combine the cornstarch, garlic powder, and ginger. Stir in apricot nectar. Cook and stir over medium heat until mixture is thickened and bubbly. Cook and stir for 2 minutes more. Remove saucepan from heat; stir in vinegar. Pour over cooked asparagus; toss gently to coat. Makes 4 servings.

1 pound **asparagus spears**
¾ teaspoon **cornstarch**
Dash **garlic powder**
Dash **ground ginger**
⅓ cup **apricot nectar** (½ of a 5½-ounce can)
1 tablespoon **white wine vinegar**

MEDITATE TO GOOD HEALTH ▶ MIND·BODY·SPIRIT

Practicing Transcendental Meditation (TM), an Eastern form of stress relief, might reduce your risk of a heart attack or stroke, even if you don't change your diet or exercise habits. TM might also lower your risk of hypertension. Regular practice of meditation often gives you a sense of peace, an important component of happiness.

Nutrition Facts per serving: 34 cal., 0 g total fat (0 g sat. fat), 0 mg chol., 4 mg sodium, 7 g carbo., 2 g fiber, 2 g pro. ▶ **Exchanges:** 1½ Vegetable

Nutrition Facts per serving: 85 cal., 4 g total fat (0 g sat. fat), 0 mg chol., 183 mg sodium, 13 g carbo., 5 g fiber, 3 g pro. ▶ Exchanges: 2 Vegetable, 1 Fat

2 teaspoons sesame seed

2 teaspoons olive oil or cooking oil

¼ to ½ teaspoon anise seed or caraway seed

¼ teaspoon salt

¼ teaspoon black pepper

2 cups sliced bok choy

1½ cups halved Brussels sprouts or one 10-ounce package frozen Brussels sprouts, thawed and halved

2 medium carrots, bias-sliced

2 tablespoons water

1 tablespoon lemon juice

In a 1-cup glass measure combine sesame seed, oil, anise seed or caraway seed, salt, and pepper. Cover with waxed paper; microwave on 100 percent power (high) for 3 to 4 minutes or until sesame seed is lightly toasted, stirring once. Set mixture aside.

In a 1½-quart microwave-safe casserole combine bok choy, Brussels sprouts, and carrots; add water. Cover and microwave on high for 6 to 8 minutes or until crisp-tender, stirring once. Drain.

Stir lemon juice into sesame seed mixture; pour over vegetables. Toss gently to coat. Makes 4 servings.

This recipe is perfect alongside roasted meat or poultry.
Don't worry about being short on oven space—it cooks in the microwave.

lemon-sesame vegetables

CHAPTER SEVEN

no-guilt des

serts

Nutrition Facts per serving: 137 cal., 2 g total fat (0 g sat. fat), 0 mg chol., 92 mg sodium, 28 g carbo., 1 g fiber, 2 g pro. ▶ Exchanges: 1 Starch, ½ Fruit, ½ Fat

3 medium **peaches, peeled, pitted, and coarsely chopped, or 2¼ cups frozen unsweetened peach slices, thawed and coarsely chopped**

2 tablespoons **granulated sugar**

4 teaspoons **miniature semisweet chocolate pieces**

1 tablespoon **all-purpose flour**

1 teaspoon **lemon juice**

Nonstick cooking spray

4 sheets **frozen phyllo dough (18×14-inch rectangles), thawed**

2 teaspoons **powdered sugar**

Fresh raspberries (optional)

For filling, in a medium bowl combine peaches, granulated sugar, chocolate pieces, flour, and lemon juice. Toss to combine; set aside.

Lightly coat four 6-ounce custard cups with nonstick cooking spray; set aside. Lightly coat 1 phyllo sheet with nonstick spray. (Keep remaining phyllo sheets covered with a damp cloth to keep them from drying out.) Place another sheet of phyllo on top of the first sheet; lightly coat with nonstick spray. Repeat twice. Cut stack in half lengthwise and in half crosswise, forming 4 rectangles.

Gently ease one stack of phyllo into bottom and up the sides of one custard cup (phyllo will hang over edge). Spoon about ½ cup of the peach filling into center. Bring phyllo up over filling, pinching together to form a ruffled edge. Lightly coat again with nonstick spray. Repeat with remaining cups, phyllo, and filling. Place custard cups in a 15×10×1-inch baking pan.

Bake in a 375° oven for 20 minutes. Cool 5 minutes in custard cups; remove from cups. Serve warm or cool. Sift powdered sugar over pastry tops before serving. If desired, garnish with fresh raspberries and peach slices. Makes 4 servings.

Frozen Peaches Tip: If using frozen peaches, blot them well with paper towels after thawing to remove excess moisture.

Phyllo dough, low in calories and fat, creates a delicate shell for a peach and chocolate filling.

peach-filled phyllo bundles

glazed strawberry pie

Luscious, juicy berries pack this classic pie. Serve topped with a spoonful of light whipped dessert topping for a well-deserved treat.

Prepare Oil Pastry for Single-Crust Pie; prick bottom and sides of pastry generously with the tines of a fork. Bake in a 450° oven for 10 to 12 minutes or until pastry is golden. Cool on a wire rack.

Place 1 cup of the strawberries and the water in a food processor bowl. Cover; process until smooth. Transfer to a small saucepan. Bring to boiling; simmer for 2 minutes.

In a medium saucepan stir together sugar and cornstarch; stir in berry mixture. Cook and stir over medium heat until bubbly. Cook and stir for 2 minutes more. Remove from heat; stir in enough red food coloring to tint a rich red color. Cool to room temperature.

Fold remaining strawberries into cooled mixture; pour into pastry shell. Cover; chill for 3 to 4 hours. If desired, serve with whipped topping. Makes 8 servings.

Oil Pastry for Single-Crust Pie: In a bowl stir together 1¼ cups all-purpose flour and ¼ teaspoon salt. Combine ¼ cup fat-free milk and 3 tablespoons cooking oil. Add milk mixture all at once to flour mixture. Stir with a fork until dough forms; form into a ball. On a lightly floured surface slightly flatten dough. Roll dough into a 12-inch circle. Ease pastry into a 9-inch pie plate. Trim pastry to ½ inch beyond edge of plate. Fold under extra pastry; crimp edge as desired.

1 recipe Oil Pastry for Single-Crust Pie

6 cups strawberries

1 cup water

¼ cup sugar

2 tablespoons cornstarch

Few drops red food coloring

Fat-free frozen whipped dessert topping, thawed (optional)

Nutrition Facts per serving: 179 cal., 6 g total fat (1 g sat. fat), 0 mg chol., 73 mg sodium, 30 g carbo., 3 g fiber, 3 g pro. ▶ Exchanges: 1½ Starch, ½ Fruit, 1 Fat

Nutrition Facts per serving: **161** cal., **1** g total fat (0 g sat. fat), 0 mg chol., 113 mg sodium, 34 g carbo., 0 g fiber, 4 g pro. ▶ Exchanges: 1 Starch, 1 Fruit

Nonstick spray coating

8 sheets frozen phyllo dough (about 18×14-inch rectangles), thawed

¼ cup finely crushed gingersnap cookies

⅔ cup sugar

1 envelope unflavored gelatin

1½ cups water

½ teaspoon finely shredded lemon peel

¼ cup lemon juice

Few drops yellow food coloring (optional)

1 1.3-ounce envelope whipped dessert topping mix

½ cup fat-free milk

Fresh raspberries, kiwifruit slices, and lemon peels

Lightly coat a 10½-inch round tart pan with a removable bottom with nonstick cooking spray. Cut phyllo in half to make sixteen 14-inch squares. Keep phyllo covered with a damp cloth. Place 1 phyllo sheet in prepared pan; allow ends to hang over edge. Lightly coat with nonstick spray. Sprinkle with gingersnap crumbs. Add another sheet of phyllo, staggering corners. Repeat with remaining phyllo, cooking spray, and crumbs, ending with phyllo and cooking spray. Trim phyllo to 2 inches beyond rim of pan. Fold edges toward center, forming a shallow edge. Lightly press center of phyllo in pan to remove bubbles. Line with a double thickness of foil. Place on a baking sheet. Bake in a 375° oven for 10 minutes. Remove foil; bake for 5 to 7 minutes more or until golden. Cool.

For filling, in a heavy small saucepan combine sugar and gelatin; stir in water. Cook and stir over low heat until gelatin is dissolved. Remove from heat; stir in lemon peel, lemon juice, and, if desired, food coloring. Pour into a bowl. Cover; refrigerate for 1 hour or until mixture has the consistency of corn syrup, stirring occasionally.

Prepare topping mix according to package directions, except use the ½ cup milk. Fold partially set gelatin into topping. Cover; refrigerate for 1 hour or until mixture mounds when spooned. Spoon into cooled crust. Cover; chill for 2 to 6 hours or until firm. Top with raspberries, kiwifruit slices, and lemon peel twists. Makes 10 servings.

Combine a light lemon filling with a crisp phyllo dough crust for an ethereal dessert.

lemon-phyllo fruit tart

raspberry cake

Raspberries dot the filling of this easy-to-make cake. Enjoy a piece with a cup of tea or coffee for a relaxing afternoon snack.

Nonstick spray coating

1 cup fresh or frozen raspberries

1 cup all-purpose flour

1 cup sugar

1 teaspoon baking powder

¼ cup margarine or butter, melted

½ cup refrigerated or frozen egg product, thawed

2 teaspoons vanilla

1 8-ounce container plain fat-free yogurt

2 tablespoons all-purpose flour

1½ teaspoons finely shredded lemon peel

Spray a 9-inch springform pan with nonstick coating; set aside. Thaw frozen raspberries, if using, at room temperature for 15 minutes. Drain thawed berries.

In a medium bowl combine the 1 cup flour, ½ cup of the sugar, and baking powder. Add melted margarine or butter, ¼ cup of the egg product, and 1 teaspoon of the vanilla; stir until combined. Spread onto bottom of prepared pan; sprinkle with raspberries.

In a medium mixing bowl combine the yogurt, remaining ½ cup sugar, remaining ¼ cup egg product, the 2 tablespoons flour, lemon peel, and the remaining 1 teaspoon vanilla. Stir until smooth; pour over berries.

Bake in a 350° oven about 35 minutes or until center appears set when shaken gently. Cool in pan on a wire rack for 15 minutes. Loosen and remove sides of pan; cool completely. Cover and chill for 2 to 24 hours before serving. Makes 12 servings.

Nutrition Facts per serving: 164 cal., 4 g total fat (1 g sat. fat), 1 mg chol., 107 mg sodium, 28 g carbo., 1 g fiber, 4 g pro. ▶ Exchanges: 1½ Starch, ½ Fat

Nutrition Facts per serving: 152 cal., 3 g total fat (1 g sat. fat), 72 mg chol., 73 mg sodium, 27 g carbo., 1 g fiber, 4 g pro. ▶ Exchanges: 1½ Starch, ½ Fat

Nonstick spray coating

1 **mango, peeled, seeded, and chopped**

⅔ cup **sugar**

¼ cup **all-purpose flour**

Dash **salt**

2 tablespoons **lemon juice**

1 tablespoon **margarine or butter, melted**

3 **egg yolks**

1 8-ounce carton **low-fat lemon yogurt**

½ cup **fat-free milk**

3 **egg whites**

Mango wedges and/or raspberries (optional)

Lightly coat a 2-quart square baking dish with nonstick cooking spray; arrange chopped mango in the bottom of the dish. Set aside.

In a large bowl combine sugar, flour, and salt; stir in lemon juice and melted margarine or butter. In a medium bowl beat egg yolks thoroughly with a rotary beater; beat in yogurt and milk. Add to lemon mixture; stir to combine.

In a medium mixing bowl beat egg whites with an electric mixer on medium speed about 1 minute or until soft peaks form. Beat on high speed until stiff peaks form; fold into lemon mixture. Carefully spoon batter over mango in prepared dish.

Place baking dish in a larger pan on the oven rack. Pour hot water into larger pan around baking dish to a depth of 1 inch. Bake in a 350° oven about 40 minutes or until set. Cool on a wire rack for 30 minutes. Serve warm. If desired, garnish each serving with mango and/or raspberries. Makes 9 servings.

lemon-mango pudding cake

The scent of this fruit-filled cake will whet your appetite as it bakes. Fortunately, you don't have to wait until it cools to enjoy.

Nutrition Facts per serving: 173 cal., 3 g total fat (1 g sat. fat), 5 mg chol., 136 mg sodium, 36 g carbo., 1 g fiber, 1 g pro. ▶ Exchanges: 1½ Starch, ½ Fruit, ½ Fat

¼ cup low-fat cinnamon graham cracker crumbs

1 tablespoon granulated sugar

2 sheets frozen phyllo dough (18×14-inch rectangles), thawed

Nonstick spray coating

1 tablespoon margarine or butter

1 tablespoon brown sugar

3 medium apples, peeled, cored, and thinly sliced

¼ cup raisins or dried cherries

1 tablespoon apple brandy or water

¼ teaspoon ground cinnamon

⅛ teaspoon ground nutmeg

⅓ cup fat-free caramel ice cream topping

Ground cinnamon (optional)

Fresh mint (optional)

In a small bowl combine graham cracker crumbs and sugar; set aside.

Cut phyllo sheets in half crosswise. Lightly coat phyllo halves with nonstick cooking spray. Sprinkle one-fourth of crumb mixture on 1 phyllo half. Top with a phyllo sheet and one-fourth of the crumb mixture; repeat with remaining phyllo and crumb mixture. Cut the four-layer stack into nine 2¾×4-inch rectangles. Cut each rectangle diagonally in half to form 2 triangles (18 triangles total). Lightly coat a large baking sheet with nonstick cooking spray. Carefully place triangles on baking sheet. Bake in a 375° oven for 6 to 8 minutes or until golden brown.

Meanwhile, in a large skillet melt margarine or butter; stir in brown sugar. Stir in apples, raisins or cherries, brandy, cinnamon, nutmeg, and 3 tablespoons of the ice cream topping. Cook, uncovered, about 5 minutes or until apples are tender, stirring occasionally.

To serve, place a strudel triangle on each of 6 dessert plates. Spoon one-third of apple mixture over each triangle. Add a second strudel triangle. Top with half of the remaining apple mixture. Repeat with remaining triangles and apple mixture. Drizzle with remaining ice cream topping. If desired, sprinkle with cinnamon; garnish with mint. Serve immediately. Makes 6 servings.

Thin, crisp layers of oven-toasted phyllo topped with slices of spiced caramel apples will garner rave reviews.

strudel triangles with apples

baked pears with almond crunch

Pears baked in wine take on a wonderful flavor. A simple sprinkling of amaretti cookies supplies a satisfying crunch.

Place pear halves, cut sides up, in a 2-quart square baking dish. Pour wine over pears. In a small bowl combine crushed cookies, brown sugar, and cinnamon; sprinkle over pears.

Bake, uncovered, in a 350° oven for 20 minutes or until pears are tender.

Serve pears warm or at room temperature. If desired, top pears with low-fat ice cream. Makes 4 servings.

Wine Tip: When choosing a sweet wine for this recipe, look for late harvest Riesling, Sauternes, Madeira, sherry, or port (which will give the pears a ruby red color).

2 medium ripe but firm pears, peeled, halved, and cored

½ cup sweet white wine

½ cup slightly crushed amaretti cookies (crisp almond-flavored macaroons)

1 tablespoon brown sugar

⅛ teaspoon ground cinnamon

Low-fat ice cream (optional)

THE RIGHT SCENT ▶ MIND·BODY·SPIRIT

You can trigger desirable emotions according to the fragrance you choose. Although scientists debate whether aromatherapy has specific healing properties, there's little doubt certain aromas can help you recall pleasant experiences. Try smelling your mother's perfume or your father's cologne—it could help induce feelings of security or comfort.

Nutrition Facts per serving: **229** cal., 6 g total fat (0 g sat. fat), 0 mg chol., 9 mg sodium, 42 g carbo., 5 g fiber, 2 g pro. ▶ Exchanges: 2 Starch, ½ Fruit, 1 Fat

Nutrition Facts per serving: 277 cal., 9 g total fat (5 g sat. fat), 45 mg chol., 186 mg sodium, 45 g carbo., 2 g fiber, 5 g pro. ▶ Exchanges: 3 Starch, 1 Fat

Nonstick cooking spray

1½ cups all-purpose flour

½ cup granulated sugar

¼ cup packed brown sugar

1 teaspoon baking powder

¼ teaspoon baking soda

½ cup mashed ripe banana (1 large)

⅓ cup fat-free dairy sour cream

⅓ cup butter or margarine, softened

½ teaspoon vanilla

1 egg

2 egg whites

1 cup fresh or frozen blueberries

1 recipe Crumb Topping

Lightly coat an 11×7×2-inch or 8×8×2-inch baking pan with nonstick cooking spray; set aside. In a medium mixing bowl combine flour, granulated sugar, brown sugar, baking powder, and baking soda. Add banana, sour cream, butter or margarine, and vanilla. Beat with an electric mixer on low to medium speed until combined. Add egg and egg whites; beat for 1 minute more. Fold in blueberries. Pour batter into prepared pan, spreading evenly. Sprinkle with Crumb Topping.

Bake in a 350° oven about 45 minutes or until a wooden toothpick inserted near the center comes out clean. Serve warm or cool completely in pan on a wire rack. Makes 9 servings.

Crumb Topping: In a small bowl combine ¼ cup rolled oats; 3 tablespoons brown sugar; 2 tablespoons all-purpose flour; 1 tablespoon butter or margarine, melted; and ¼ teaspoon ground cinnamon. Stir until crumbly.

Replace some of the fat—but none of the flavor—by using mashed banana in this crumb-topped snack cake.

blueberry-banana cake

chocolate ice cream roll

This do-ahead dessert is spectacular enough to serve as a grand finale to your most elegant dinner. (P.S. Kids will like it, too.)

Grease and flour a 15×10×1-inch baking pan. In a large bowl stir together flour, cocoa powder, baking powder, and salt. Set aside. In a small mixing bowl beat egg yolks and vanilla with an electric mixer on high speed for 5 minutes or until lemon-colored. Gradually add the ⅓ cup sugar, beating on medium speed about 5 minutes or until sugar is almost dissolved. Wash and dry beaters.

In a large mixing bowl beat egg whites on high speed until soft peaks form. Add the ½ cup sugar, beating until stiff peaks form. Fold yolk mixture into egg white mixture. Sprinkle flour mixture over egg mixture; fold in gently. Spread batter into prepared pan. Bake in a 375° oven for 12 to 15 minutes or until top springs. Loosen edges of hot cake from pan; turn out onto a clean dish towel sprinkled with powdered sugar. Starting with a narrow end, roll up cake and towel together. Cool.

Unroll cake. Spread ice cream onto cake to within 1 inch of edges. Sprinkle with pecans. Reroll cake without towel. Wrap and freeze at least 4 hours. To serve, if desired, drizzle Raspberry Sauce over serving plates. Slice cake; place slices on plates. If desired, garnish with berries and mint. Serves 10.

Raspberry Sauce: In a small saucepan heat ⅔ cup seedless raspberry spreadable fruit, 1 tablespoon lemon juice, and ¼ teaspoon almond extract until spreadable fruit is melted. Cool slightly.

⅓ cup **all-purpose flour**

¼ cup **unsweetened cocoa powder**

1 teaspoon **baking powder**

¼ teaspoon **salt**

4 **egg yolks**

½ teaspoon **vanilla**

⅓ cup **granulated sugar**

4 **egg whites**

½ cup **granulated sugar**

Sifted **powdered sugar**

1 quart **fat-free vanilla ice cream, softened**

¼ cup **broken pecans, toasted**

1 recipe **Raspberry Sauce (optional)**

Fresh raspberries (optional)

Fresh mint (optional)

Nutrition Facts per serving: 211 cal., 5 g total fat (1 g sat. fat), 85 mg chol., 171 mg sodium, 38 g carbo., 0 g fiber, 6 g pro. ▶ Exchanges: 2½ Starch, ½ Fat

chocolate-cream cheese cupcakes

Not just for breakfast, granola adds a low-fat crunch to the top of these chocolate cupcakes.

½ of an 8-ounce package fat-free cream cheese, softened

1⅓ cup sugar

¼ cup refrigerated or frozen egg product, thawed

⅓ cup miniature semisweet chocolate pieces

1½ cups all-purpose flour

¼ cup unsweetened cocoa powder

1 teaspoon baking powder

¼ teaspoon baking soda

⅛ teaspoon salt

1 cup water

⅓ cup cooking oil

1 tablespoon vinegar

1 teaspoon vanilla

½ cup low-fat granola

Line 18 muffin cups with paper bake cups; set aside.

In a small mixing bowl beat cream cheese with an electric mixer on medium speed until smooth. Add ⅓ cup of the sugar and the egg product. Beat on medium speed for 1 minute or until smooth. Stir in the semisweet chocolate pieces; set aside.

In a large mixing bowl combine remaining 1 cup sugar, the flour, cocoa powder, baking powder, baking soda, and salt. Add water, oil, vinegar, and vanilla. Beat with an electric mixer on medium speed for 2 minutes, scraping sides of bowl occasionally. Spoon batter into the prepared muffin cups, filling each half full. Spoon about 1 tablespoon of the cream cheese mixture over each. Sprinkle with granola.

Bake in a 350° oven for 25 to 30 minutes or until tops spring back when lightly touched. Cool cupcakes in pan on a wire rack for 10 minutes. Remove cupcakes from pan; cool thoroughly on wire rack. Makes 18 cupcakes.

Nutrition Facts per cupcake: 166 cal., 5 g total fat (1 g sat. fat), 1 mg chol., 62 mg sodium, 27 g carbo., 0 g fiber, 3 g pro. ▶ Exchanges: 1½ Starch, 1 Fat

Nutrition Facts per serving: 172 cal., 5 g total fat (1 g sat. fat), 24 mg chol., 117 mg sodium, 30 g carbo., 2 g fiber, 3 g pro. ▶ Exchanges: 1 Starch, 1 Fruit, 1 Fat

1 cup **all-purpose flour**

¼ cup **sugar**

1½ teaspoons **baking powder**

1 teaspoon **finely shredded orange peel**

½ teaspoon **ground cinnamon**

3 tablespoons **margarine or butter**

1 16-ounce package **frozen unsweetened pitted tart red cherries**

4 teaspoons **cornstarch**

½ teaspoon **ground cinnamon**

3 to 4 medium **pears** (1 pound), peeled, cored, and thinly sliced (3 cups)

1 **egg**

¼ cup **fat-free milk**

Fat-free frozen yogurt (optional)

For biscuit topping, in a medium bowl stir together flour, 2 tablespoons of the sugar, the baking powder, orange peel, and cinnamon. Cut in margarine or butter until mixture resembles coarse crumbs. Set aside.

For filling, in a medium saucepan combine frozen cherries and ¼ cup water, the remaining 2 tablespoons sugar, cornstarch, and cinnamon. Cook and stir until thickened and bubbly. Stir in pear slices; heat through. Reduce heat; keep hot.

In a bowl stir together egg and milk; add to topping mixture, stirring just until moistened. Transfer hot filling to a 2-quart square baking dish. Immediately spoon topping mixture into small mounds over filling. Bake in a 400° oven for 20 to 25 minutes or until a wooden toothpick inserted near center of a biscuit comes out clean. If desired, serve cobbler warm with frozen yogurt. Makes 9 servings.

pear and cherry cobbler

Nothing is more welcome than the old-fashioned goodness of hot fruit covered with a cinnamon-scented biscuit dough.

Nutrition Facts per serving: 150 cal., 2 g total fat (1 g sat. fat), 55 mg chol., 56 mg sodium, 29 g carbo., 4 g fiber, 5 g pro. ▶ Exchanges: 3 Starch, ½ Meat

¼ cup sugar

2 teaspoons cornstarch

1 cup fat-free milk

1 beaten egg

2 tablespoons light dairy sour cream

½ teaspoon vanilla

3 cups fresh raspberries, blackberries, blueberries, or halved strawberries

For custard, in a small saucepan thoroughly combine 2 tablespoons of the sugar and the cornstarch; add the milk and egg. Cook and stir with a wooden spoon over medium heat just until the mixture begins to bubble. (Do not overcook.) Immediately pour the custard into a small bowl; let mixture cool about 5 minutes.

Whisk sour cream into custard; add vanilla. Cover and chill custard for up to 24 hours.

To serve, divide berries evenly among four goblets or dessert dishes. Spoon chilled custard over berries. (If necessary, thin custard with a little milk before spooning over berries.) Set aside.

For topping, in a small heavy skillet or saucepan heat remaining 2 tablespoons sugar over medium-high heat until sugar begins to melt, shaking skillet occasionally to heat evenly (do not stir). Reduce heat to low; cook sugar until melted and golden, stirring as necessary with a wooden spoon. Quickly drizzle caramelized sugar over each custard. Serve immediately. Makes 4 servings.

Layers of raspberries and custard topped with lacy caramelized sugar form this elegant yet easy-to-make dessert.

raspberry custard brûlée

Nutrition Facts per serving: 287 cal., 4 g total fat (1 g sat. fat), 161 mg chol., 100 mg sodium, 55 g carbo., 1 g fiber, 8 g pro. ▶ Exchanges: 1½ Starch

⅔ cup **sugar**

¾ cup **refrigerated or frozen egg product, thawed**

¾ cup **canned pumpkin**

1 5-ounce can (⅔ cup) **evaporated fat-free milk**

¼ cup **sugar**

1 teaspoon **pumpkin pie spice**

1 teaspoon **finely shredded orange peel**

1 teaspoon **vanilla**

To caramelize sugar, in a heavy medium skillet heat the ⅔ cup sugar over medium-high heat until sugar begins to melt, shaking skillet occasionally to heat evenly (do not stir). Reduce heat to low; cook sugar until melted and golden brown, stirring as necessary with a wooden spoon. Quickly divide caramelized sugar among four 6-ounce custard cups; tilt cups to coat bottoms evenly.

Place custard cups in a 3-quart rectangular baking pan. In a medium bowl stir together egg product, pumpkin, evaporated milk, the ¼ cup sugar, pumpkin pie spice, orange peel, and vanilla. Pour pumpkin mixture over caramelized sugar in cups. Place pan on oven rack. Pour boiling water into pan around cups to a depth of 1 inch. Bake in a 325° oven for 40 to 45 minutes or until a knife inserted near the centers comes out clean. Remove cups from pan. Cool slightly. Cover; refrigerate for 4 to 24 hours.

To serve, loosen edges of flans with a knife, slipping the point down the sides to let air in. Invert flans onto four dessert plates, spooning caramelized sugar onto flans. Makes 4 servings.

Forget plain flan. This recipe adds flair and flavor with pumpkin pie spice and orange peel.

citrus pumpkin flan

baked rice pudding

Old-fashioned rice pudding deserves a place in your recipe box. But this version adds a slight twist to a favorite with apricot and orange.

In a medium mixing bowl combine egg whites, egg, milk, sugar, and vanilla. Beat until combined but not foamy. Stir in cooked rice, apricots and/or raisins, and, if desired, orange peel. Pour rice mixture into a 1½-quart casserole. Place casserole in a baking pan on an oven rack. Pour boiling water into the baking pan around the casserole to a depth of 1 inch.

Bake, uncovered, in a 325° oven for 45 to 55 minutes or until just set, stirring after 35 minutes. Serve warm or chilled. If desired, garnish with apricot slices and sprinkle with cinnamon. Makes 5 servings.

MIND·BODY·SPIRIT ▶ A FRIEND IN NEED

Did you know that loneliness can cause serious health consequences? A study of 37,000 people found that those who lived alone or had few friends were more likely to die over a decade of time than those who had friends and frequent social contacts. Having close friends also seems to hinder stress-related deterioration of the immune system.

3 egg whites

1 egg

1½ cups fat-free milk

¼ cup sugar

1 teaspoon vanilla

⅔ cup cooked rice

2 tablespoons snipped dried apricots and/or light raisins

¼ teaspoon finely shredded orange peel (optional)

Sliced apricots (optional)

Ground cinnamon (optional)

Nutrition Facts per serving: **136** cal., 1 g total fat (0 g sat. fat), 44 mg chol., 84 mg sodium, 24 g carbo., 0 g fiber, 7 g pro. ▶ Exchanges: 1½ Starch, ½ Fat

Nutrition Facts per serving: 172 cal., 2 g total fat (0 g sat. fat), 1 mg chol., 205 mg sodium, 31 g carbo., 1 g fiber, 8 g pro. ▶ Exchanges: 1 Starch, ½ Fruit, ½ Meat

2¼ cups fat-free milk

1 8-ounce carton
     refrigerated or frozen
     egg product, thawed

⅓ cup sugar

1 teaspoon vanilla

5 cups torn dry bread
     pieces (7 to 8 slices)

8 dried apricot halves,
     quartered

3 tablespoons dried
     currants

2 tablespoons sugar

¼ teaspoon ground
     cardamom

   Powdered sugar
     (optional)

In a medium bowl beat together milk, egg product, the ⅓ cup sugar, and vanilla. Combine bread pieces, apricots, and currants; place in a greased 10-inch round quiche dish. Pour milk mixture evenly over bread mixture in quiche dish.

For topping, stir together the 2 tablespoons sugar and cardamom. Sprinkle over bread mixture.

Bake in a 325° oven for 35 to 40 minutes or until a knife inserted near the center comes out clean. If desired, sprinkle with powdered sugar. Serve pudding warm. Makes 6 to 8 servings.

A hint of cardamom gives this dessert newfound appeal. Use "stale" bread or let fresh bread stand loosely covered on the counter for a day.

apricot bread pudding

chocolate bread pudding soufflés

As with most soufflés, these show-stopping chocolate desserts should be served as soon as they come out of the oven.

To attach foil collars to eight 5-ounce soufflé dishes, fold eight 12×4-inch strips of foil in half lengthwise. Lightly coat one side of each strip with nonstick cooking spray; sprinkle each with ¼ teaspoon sugar. Place collars around ungreased soufflé dishes, sugar side toward the center, extending 1 inch above dishes. Secure with tape or a piece of 100-percent-cotton string. Set soufflé dishes aside.

In a medium bowl stir together the ¼ cup sugar, cocoa powder, and cinnamon; add ⅔ cup of the milk and vanilla. Stir in bread cubes; set aside.

In a small saucepan melt margarine or butter. Stir in the flour. Add remaining ⅔ cup milk. Cook and stir until thickened and bubbly. Remove from heat. In a large mixing bowl beat egg yolks for 5 minutes or until thick and lemon-colored. Gradually stir in flour mixture; stir in bread mixture.

Wash beaters thoroughly. In a large mixing bowl beat egg whites until soft peaks form (tips curl). Gradually add the 3 tablespoons sugar, beating until stiff peaks form (tips stand straight). Fold bread mixture into beaten egg whites. Divide among prepared soufflé dishes.

Bake in a 350° oven for 20 to 25 minutes or until a knife inserted near centers comes out clean. Serve immediately. Makes 8 servings.

Nonstick cooking spray

Sugar

¼ cup sugar

3 tablespoons unsweetened cocoa powder

½ teaspoon ground cinnamon

1⅓ cup fat-free milk

½ teaspoon vanilla

1½ cups dry French bread cubes (crusts removed)

1 tablespoon margarine or butter

2 tablespoons all-purpose flour

3 egg yolks

3 egg whites

3 tablespoons sugar

Nutrition Facts per serving: 153 cal., 4 g total fat (1 g sat. fat), 81 mg chol., 137 mg sodium, 23 g carbo., 0 g fiber, 6 g pro. ▶ Exchanges: 1½ Starch, ½ Fat

strawberry gelato

Who can resist this creamy, sweet Italian ice cream-like dessert? It's especially good when made with fresh summer strawberries.

In a medium saucepan combine milk, egg product, and sugar. Cook and stir over medium heat about 10 minutes or until mixture is thickened. Do not boil. Remove saucepan from heat.

Place saucepan in a sink or bowl of ice water for 1 to 2 minutes, stirring constantly. Pour custard mixture into a bowl; set aside.

Place strawberries in a blender container or food processor bowl. Cover and blend or process until nearly smooth. Stir the strawberries and lemon juice into custard mixture. Cover the surface of custard with plastic wrap. Refrigerate for several hours or overnight until completely chilled. (Or to chill quickly, place bowl in a sink of ice water.)

Freeze mixture in a 2- or 3-quart ice cream freezer according to the manufacturer's directions. If desired, serve with additional fresh strawberries and garnish with oregano. Makes about fourteen ½-cup servings.

Peach Gelato-Style Dessert: Prepare as above, except substitute 4 cups cut-up, pitted, and peeled peaches (5 to 6 peaches) for the strawberries.

2 cups reduced-fat milk

1 cup refrigerated or frozen egg product, thawed

½ cup sugar

4 cups strawberries

1 teaspoon lemon juice

Fresh strawberries (optional)

Fresh oregano (optional)

Nutrition Facts per serving: 65 cal., 1 g total fat (0 g sat. fat), 3 mg chol., 41 mg sodium, 12 g carbo., 1 g fiber, 3 g pro. ▶ Exchanges: ½ Fruit, ½ Milk

2¾ cups **water**

¼ cup **sugar**

1½ cups **lightly packed fresh mint leaves**

½ of a 12-ounce can (¾ cup) frozen tangerine juice-blend concentrate, thawed

1 teaspoon finely shredded lemon peel

Mint leaves (optional)

In a small saucepan combine water and sugar. Cook and stir until sugar is dissolved. Remove from heat. Stir in the 1½ cups mint leaves. Cover and let stand for 10 minutes. Strain into a large bowl; discard mint leaves. Stir concentrate and lemon peel into strained mixture. Refrigerate for 1 to 2 hours or until chilled.

Freeze in a 2-quart ice cream freezer according to the manufacturer's directions. Ripen for 4 hours. (Or, transfer mixture to a nonmetal freezer container. Cover and freeze for 4 to 6 hours or until almost firm. Break frozen mixture into small chunks; transfer to a chilled bowl. Beat with an electric mixer until smooth but not melted. Return to container. Cover and freeze about 6 hours or until firm.)

To serve, scoop into 4 dessert dishes. If desired, garnish with mint leaves. Makes eight ½-cup servings.

This refreshing dessert can also be served as a palate cleanser between courses to give your next dinner party added panache.

minted tangerine sorbet

index

By making a few conversions, cooks in Australia, Canada, and the United Kingdom can use the recipes in this book with confidence. The charts on this page provide a guide for converting measurements from the U.S. customary system, which is used throughout this book, to the imperial and metric systems. There also is a conversion table for oven temperatures to accommodate the differences in oven calibrations.

Product Differences: Most of the ingredients called for in the recipes in this cookbook are available in English-speaking countries. However, some are known by different names. Here are some common U.S. American ingredients and their possible counterparts:

- Sugar is granulated or castor sugar.
- Powdered sugar is icing sugar.
- All-purpose flour is plain household flour or white four. When self-rising flour is used in place of all-purpose flour in a recipe that calls for leavening, omit the leavening agent (baking soda or baking powder) and salt.
- Light-colored corn syrup is golden syrup.
- Cornstarch is cornflour.
- Baking soda is bicarbonate of soda.
- Vanilla is vanilla essence.
- Green, red, or yellow sweet peppers are capsicums.
- Golden raisins are sultanas.

Volume and Weight: U.S. Americans traditionally use cup measures for liquid and solid ingredients. The chart, below, shows the approximate imperial and metric equivalents. If you are accustomed to weighing solid ingredients, the following approximate equivalents will help.

- 1 cup butter, castor sugar, or rice = 8 ounces = about 230 grams
- 1 cup flour = 4 ounces = about 115 grams
- 1 cup icing sugar = 5 ounces = about 140 grams

Spoon measures are used for smaller amounts of ingredients. Although the size of the tablespoon varies slightly in different countries, for practical purposes and for recipes in this book, a straight substitution is all that's necessary.

Measurements made using cups or spoons always should be made level unless stated otherwise.

Equivalents: U.S. = Australia/U.K.

⅕ teaspoon = 1 ml	½ cup = 120 ml
¼ teaspoon = 1.25 ml	⅔ cup = 160 ml
½ teaspoon = 2.5 ml	¾ cup = 180 ml
1 teaspoon = 5 ml	1 cup = 240 ml
1 tablespoon = 15 ml	2 cups = 475 ml
1 fluid ounce = 30 ml	1 quart = 1 liter
¼ cup = 60 ml	½ inch = 1.25 cm
⅓ cup = 80 ml	1 inch = 2.5 cm

Baking Pan Sizes

U.S.	METRIC
8x1½-inch round baking pan	20x4-cm cake tin
9x1½-inch round baking pan	23x4-cm cake tin
11x7x1½-inch baking pan	28x18x4-cm baking tin
13x9x2-inch baking pan	32x23x5-cm baking tin
2-quart rectangular baking dish	28x18x4-cm baking tin
15x10x1-inch baking pan	38x25.5x2.5-cm baking tin (Swiss roll tin)
9-inch pie plate	22x4- or 23x4-cm pie plate
7- or 8-inch springform pan	18- or 20-cm springform or loose-bottom cake tin
9x5x3-inch loaf pan	23x13x8-cm or 2-pound narrow loaf tin or pâté tin
1½-quart casserole	1.5-liter casserole

Oven Temperature Equivalents

FAHRENHEIT SETTING	CELSIUS SETTING*	GAS SETTING
300°F	150°C	Gas mark 2 (very low)
325°F	170°C	Gas mark 3 (low)
350°F	180°C	Gas mark 4 (moderate)
375°F	190°C	Gas mark 5 (moderately hot)
400°F	200°C	Gas mark 6 (hot)
425°F	220°C	Gas mark 7 (hot)
450°F	230°C	Gas mark 8 (very hot)
475°F	240°C	Gas mark 9 (very hot)
Broil		Grill

*Electric and gas ovens may be calibrated using Celsius. However, for an electric oven, increase the Celsius setting 10 to 20 degrees when cooking above 160°C. For convection or forced-air ovens (gas or electric), lower the temperature setting 10°C when cooking at all heat levels.